Creation and the Second Coming

Her

Master
Books

First printing: September 1991
Fourth printing: August 2005

ISBN: 0-89051-163-2

Cataloguing in Publication Data

I. Morris, Henry Madison, 1918–
    Creation and the Second Coming
    1. Prophecy. 2. Religion. I. Title

Cover art by Lloyd R. Hight

Printed in the United States of America.

For information regarding author interviews, please contact the publicity department at (870) 438-5288.

Master
Books
A Division of New Leaf Press
www.masterbooks.net

Table of Contents

Foreword

The casual reader of the Bible may believe that prophetic events yet unfulfilled are addressed only rarely in Scripture (e.g., Daniel, Matthew, Revelation). But the Word of God is a unified whole, depicting history as moving toward a cosmic catastrophe and the creation of a new heaven and a new earth.

To understand this climax and the prophecies that relate to it requires that we begin at the beginning—the Book of Genesis. We cannot hope to understand the work of God at the climax of history unless we understand His work at the beginning of history. Thus, any meaningful discussion of the establishment of a new world order requires an understanding of how and why God established the present world order.

Why would a renowned creation scientist write a book on prophecy? The answer is that, while most such books focus solely on future events, this one fits the future into God's program for the original creation. Dr. Henry Morris shows that future events are part of Satan's long war against God. The original perfect world order was corrupted by Satan and those who joined his rebellion against God. That war has continued throughout history, and is most graphically seen today in the programs of Darwinists, occultists and other evolutionists.

Not many treatments of end-time events relate Daniel's prophecy to the science of Newton or the philosophy of Voltaire, but this one does. Not many show that the need for a new world order is entirely consistent with the second law of thermodynamics, but this one does. That is not to say that the author does not also address all the usual themes of Biblical prophecy—the beast, the false prophet, Gog and Magog, etc.—he does. But added to these is the breadth of Dr. Morris' understanding in science, history and, of course, creationism.

Creation and the Second Coming places the future in the context of God's original world order, tarnished by Satan's rebellion and man's fall. Anyone who wishes to understand the futility of man's attempts to establish his own world order will appreciate the unique insights of this book.

Woodrow Kroll, Th.D.
General Director,
Back to the Bible, Inc.

Acknowledgments

I wish to thank Dr. Richard Bliss, Dr. John Morris, and Don Rohrer for reviewing the manuscript for this book prior to its publication. Don and Rebecca Barber prepared the manuscript for printing.

I am especially grateful to Dr. Woodrow Kroll, both for reviewing the manuscript and for writing the Foreword. As General Director of the worldwide ministry of the Back-to-the-Bible organization, Dr. Kroll is one of the key Christian leaders of our day. With a Th.D. degree from St. Albans Theological Seminary in Geneva, plus further training at the Ph.D. level at Harvard, Gordon-Conwell and the University of Virginia, he is both a brilliant scholar and a warm-hearted practical teacher of God's Word. It is a privilege to count him as a personal friend and strong colleague in the defense of our Christian faith.

Introduction

In recent years, there has been much talk about a coming "new world order." Many people, in every nation, have longed for a world where peace, prosperity and freedom prevail. Americans had hoped that World War I would "make the world safe for democracy," and the League of Nations was formed to try to secure this result. Predictably, it failed, because human nature had not changed, and the Darwinian philosophy ("survival of the fittest" and "might makes right") that had led to the Great War was still being taught in the schools and colleges of the world.

The Second World War had a similar cause. Hitler and Mussolini, as well as the Chinese Communists and Japanese militarists, all operated on the basis of evolutionary and anti-Christian premises. On the other side, President Franklin D. Roosevelt eloquently championed the goals of freedom in a new world order—freedom from fear and poverty, freedom from war and oppression, as well as the traditional American freedoms guaranteed in our Bill of Rights (freedom of speech, freedom of religion, etc.). After this war, the United Nations Organization was established, amid much propaganda assuring the world of future global peace. Sir Julian Huxley, the world's leading evolutionary scientist, was appointed first Director General of its United Nations Educational, Scientific and Cultural Organization (UNESCO), with the purpose of implementing his dream of a global culture based on what he called evolutionary humanism.

Huxley and his fellow evolutionary globalists, especially the French paleontologist/priest Teilhard de Chardin, stimulated what has come to be called the "New Age" movement among scientists and other intellectuals, especially the baby-boom student generation of the sixties. This "Aquarian Conspiracy," as Marilyn Ferguson, one of its leaders, has called the movement, now embraces a wide spectrum of beliefs, practices, cults and organizations—all promoting what is essentially a revival of some form of ancient pantheistic paganism. They call it "New-Age," but it is as old as the world's rebellion against its Creator. All such groups believe in evolution and all are promoting a "new world order," as they call it. By this they mean a world government, world culture and world religion, centered in evolutionary humanistic pantheism.

In recent years, even President George Bush has been calling again and again for a new world order. No doubt he is sincere in thinking this can be achieved by political efforts, and he (hopefully) means something quite different from what the New Age globalists have in mind, but human nature *still* has not changed, and there can never be *true* world peace and freedom until the world's Creator returns to set it up Himself.

The fact is, however, that He is going to do just that, and indications abound that He will do it very soon! For the Creator of this world was none other than the Lord Jesus Christ, and, after He paid the price on the cross for our redemption, He promised to return in the "last days" to complete the actual "redemption of the purchased possession, unto the praise of His glory" (Ephesians 1:14).

Jesus Christ will, indeed, soon establish His own new world order here on Earth. The details of its accomplishment constitute a prominent theme in the Word of God. Many signs of His imminent return to begin this work are given in the prophetic Scriptures and are being fulfilled today with ever-increasing clarity.

There have been many books published on Biblical prophecy, but these books have largely ignored the significance of the first days of the world and God's purposes for the world in the understanding of the last days. The basic message of creation, in opposition to the false concept of evolution, seems to me to be vital if we are really going to understand the ultimate consummation of God's purposes in this world.

After all, we are considering the imminent return of Jesus Christ to the earth, and He is the one who created it in the first place! Once, long ago, "He was in the world, and the world was made by Him and the world knew Him not" (John 1:10). Now, after 2000 years of Christianity, His second coming is very near, yet He is still mostly unknown to this world He created. Looking forward to these times, with deep sadness, He asked rhetorically, "When the Son of Man cometh, shall He find faith on the earth?" (Luke 18:8). Paradoxically, even this widespread indifference of the world to its Creator and the pervasive rebellion of its leaders against the very concept of divine creation constitute evidence that His return is near, for all this is given in Scripture as one more sign of the last days. Many of the evidences of the last days, as outlined in Chapter 1, are directly related to God's purposes in creation and our rebellion against these purposes.

Perhaps the most eloquent and obvious sign of His coming is the boiling Middle East. These lands of the Bible, long more or less ignored by the rest of the world, have become the center ring of the great world circus. What goes around, comes around, and it almost seems as if the very stones of the "waste howling wilderness" (Deuteronomy 32:10), which characterize so much of this region, are crying out for the return of their Creator to make things new and right again. Accordingly, Chapter 2 will survey the Biblical prophecies of these latter-day conflicts in the Middle East.

Chapters 3 and 4 will focus on Jerusalem and Babylon, respectively, and the roles—both actual and symbolic—which the world's two key cities, the city of God and the city of Antichrist, will play in the last great events of this present age. They are both getting ready now, and this is still another indication that God is almost ready to step down into His rebellious Creation once again.

The great climactic period of Satan's long war against God, along with God's final judgments on him and his followers, with the accompanying cleansing of the whole creation, are described in Chapters 5 and 6. Finally, the last chapter places all these future events in proper focus for believers today, anticipating the very near return of the Lord Jesus Christ to implement and complete God's plan of the ages.

Since the future is much more difficult to know than the past, and since there are wide differences of opinion among Bible scholars on how to interpret the prophetic Scriptures, my own analysis is not intended to be dogmatic. Where the Bible speaks plainly however, we do well to take it plainly, and it surely does speak clearly concerning the reality of primeval special creation and the urgent importance of the creation message in the last days. The Lord Jesus Christ is both the Creator of the world (Colossians 1:16) and the Redeemer of the world (Colossians 1:20). Very soon now, He will finally be acknowledged as King of the world (Revelation 17:14). Therefore, like the coming angel, we must call on men to "worship Him that made heaven, and earth, and the sea" in these closing days before "the hour of His judgment is come" (Revelation 14:7).

CHAPTER 1

How we Know the End is Near

Harbingers of His Coming

The evolutionary world view (i.e., that the universe has organized itself into its present complexity by *natural* processes) that has opposed the Biblical world view throughout history assumes that the universe has existed for great ages in the past and will continue along its evolutionary path for ages yet to come—if not on Earth, then perhaps on other planets circling distant stars. Many have assumed that these endless processes occur in repeated cycles of life, death and reincarnation. Others have assumed slow development of complex life out of the primordial chaos "perhaps out of a shapeless watery mass or else a plasma of energized particles, or even some cosmic thought-field. Evolutionism has taken many forms over the ages, but has always assumed endless ages and has denied any act of real creation by a personal, transcendent God.

The Bible, on the other hand, clearly teaches that the universe was created *supernaturally*, not over long ages of evolutionary development, but very quickly in a brief series of creative acts associated with the Creator's omnipotent Word. "By the Word of the LORD were the heavens made; and all the host of them by the breath of His mouth" (Psalm 33:6). "Through faith we understand that the worlds were framed by the Word of God, so that things which are seen were not made of things which do appear" (Hebrews 11:3).

Just as it did not take long ages of evolution for God to develop His created world, so it will not take long ages for Him to prepare His redeemed world for its divinely ordained purpose in that perfect world that is to come. These thousands of years of human struggle and suffering and dying, nations rising and falling, days and years and centuries passing into forgotten history, may seem ever so long to us, but "a thousand years in thy sight are but as yesterday when it is past, and as a watch in the night" (Psalm 90:4). This is how it is in God's sight, and how it will also seem to us in eternity.

From the very beginning of human history, God has been promising a consummation of human history. His purposes in creation, interrupted and seemingly thwarted by human rebellion, will finally be accomplished, through God's great plan of redemption and salvation. This plan required God to become man; our Creator also had to become our Redeemer. He next had to die for our sins, and defeat death by His resurrection. Then, after remaining for a brief interval in heaven, He has promised to return to earth to make all things new again. The renewed earth will serve thenceforth as the eternal home of redeemed men and women. They will have been prepared on the old earth to serve their great Creator/Redeemer forever in the earth made new again.

Furthermore, just as He has recorded promises of His return in His written Word, He has included with them all needed guidance for life in our temporary abode in this present world. For we who are living in the brief interval between His first and second comings to this world, He has even recorded many indicators in His Word to let us know when we are nearing the end of the age. The exciting truth is that all these signs are coming more clearly into focus every day, so that believers everywhere are excitedly looking for their Lord's return.

We need to be careful here, of course. During the almost 2000 years since Christ first came into the world, believers in each generation have been looking for His second coming. Faulty interpretations by careless Bible students have led to setting dates for His return, and the predicted dates have all come and gone without His appearing. We are not surprised at these failures, for Christ clearly warned that "in such an hour as ye think not the Son of man cometh.... Watch therefore, for ye know neither the day nor the hour wherein the Son of man cometh" (Matthew 24:44; 25:13).

Nevertheless, the Scriptures *do* give us many signs of the approaching end, and these must be there for our under-standing and guidance. In fact, Christ, Himself, said concerning them: "When ye shall see these things come to pass, know that it is nigh, even at the doors" (Mark 13:29).

Thus, even with all allowance for possible doubtful interpretations and with all due caution against sensationalism and date-setting, these signs seem to have become so numerous and so evident all around us today that we would be foolish not to take them seriously, looking up with great joy and anticipation for the imminent return of our Lord.

The signs have been increasing in clarity for many years now. I remember my grandmother quoting an evangelist she had heard talking about Mussolini and other supposed signs of that day, predicting that Christ would return in 1933. When the atomic bomb exploded in Japan in 1945, even though I knew better than to set dates for Christ's coming, I was certain His return was so near that I almost decided not to go to graduate school. I have kept a plaque reading PERHAPS TODAY! on my office wall for almost 50 years now, and have noted that the signs which seemed so obvious 50 years ago have continued to grow in intensity with each passing year. Surely the Lord is coming soon!

It is vital, of course, that we continue to obey His command to "occupy till I come" (Luke 19:13), working in His vineyard faithfully until He *does* come. It is also vital that we "abide in Him; that when He shall appear we may have confidence and not be ashamed before Him at His coming" (I John 2:28). At the same time, we must continue daily to watch and be ready, for "unto them that look for Him shall He appear the second time without sin unto salvation"

(Hebrews 9:28). Paul has promised a "crown of righteousness" to all those who "love His appearing" (II Timothy 4:8).

In this chapter, therefore, I want to survey and summarize the most significant of the many signs which God has graciously provided in His Word to signal that Christ is coming soon. Many readers may already be familiar with these, but others may not, and it is refreshing to all of us to look again and again for that "blessed hope, and the glorious appearing of the great God and our Savior Jesus Christ" (Titus 2:13). Here, then, are some of the reasons for this quickening of our hope.

Worldwide Evolutionary Humanism

Perhaps the most important sign, though commonly neglected by other writers on prophecy, is the rise to worldwide dominance of the philosophy of evolutionary humanism. One form or another of this world view has characterized all the ancient pagan religions as well as the modern ethnic and pantheistic religions of the world (Buddhism, Hinduism, etc.), so this is nothing new. What is new is its intellectual conquest of those nations that previously have had a monotheistic worldview (Christianity, Judaism, Islam). In the last chapter written by the Apostle Peter, he foresaw this situation developing even among professing Christian nations.

Knowing this first, that there shall come in the last days scoffers, walking after their own lusts,

And saying, Where is the promise of His coming?
For since the fathers fell asleep, all things con-
tinue as they were from the beginning of the
creation (II Peter 3:3,4).

The last-days scoffers are obviously self-centered humanists, "walking after their own lusts" instead of desiring the will of God for their lives. They are also either nominal Christians or at least people who know about the "fathers" of the Christian church and "the promise of His coming" (therefore, living in a Christian environment where such things are taught). They have repudiated these teachings, however, and now even ridicule them.

The basis of this scoffing rejection of God's Word is their commitment to evolutionism. Since "all things continue as they were from the beginning of the creation," they will say, therefore, "creation" is still being accomplished by these natural processes that "continue" in the present just as they have throughout the past. "The creation" was not "finished," as God had insisted after His six days of creation (Genesis 2:1-3), but is still continuing and will continue to continue in the future, so "where is the promise of His coming?" Since there was no supernatural creation at the beginning, there will be no supernatural consummation at the ending. This is how people in Christian cultures in the last days will try to rationalize their scoffing rejection of the Word of God. "No deity will save us—we will save ourselves!" was the challenge uttered against the God of creation in the infamous Second Humanist Manifesto (1973).

This prophecy began to be fulfilled with the rise of the Lyell/Darwin evolutionary worldview in the mid-nineteenth century, and now completely dominates the schools, the colleges, the news media, the political establishment, the entertainment industry, the business world, the professions, the courts, and even the mainline churches in every nation in the so-called "Christian" world. This assertion has been thoroughly documented in my book *The Long War against God* (Baker Book House, 1989), and will be stated here simply as a known fact.

This is also true in Israel and in all the Jewish communities throughout the world, with the exception of a small minority among the Orthodox Jews. The same is true for the most part in the Muslim world, again with the exception of a minority of orthodox Muslims, and even these have a grossly distorted view of the relation between the Creator and His redemptive promises.

There can be no question that this 2000-year-old prophecy is being explicitly fulfilled today. There has, on the other hand, been a significant revival of creationism in recent decades, in many nations, but this has been a drop-in-the-bucket compared to the tidal waves of evolutionary humanism that have engulfed the world, especially among its leaders. Even though the real scientific, historical and other objective evidences all strongly support creationism and refute evolutionism (see the I.C.R. books *Scientific Creationism* and *What is Creation Science?* for example), they either ignore or distort these evidences. As Peter prophesied, they are "willingly ignorant" of the overwhelming testimony in nature and Scripture of two great supernatural worldwide events of history, the special creation of all things by the Word of God and the cataclysmic destruction of "the world that then was" by the great flood (II Peter 3:5,6). The evidences in the complex structure of all systems and the physical laws that govern them all clearly speak of special creation. The great geological formations and their fossil graveyards testify plainly of the great flood. Everywhere we look we see evidence refuting the evolutionary belief that "all things continue as they were from the beginning of creation." Yet these last-days scoffers remain willfully ignorant, just as predicted.

Surely, this is a convincing proof that we are in the last days, and Christ is coming soon!

Worldwide Moral Disintegration

Now, if God's Word is rejected when He tells us about creation, it is not surprising that His commandments also are ignored. If there is no divine Creator, or if He is so far removed from His creation in time and space as to be oblivious to it, then there is no reason why we should order our behavior by His divine standards. The worldwide capitulation to evolutionary humanism in the world's thinking has been the root cause of the worldwide collapse in moral behavior. This also is given in Scripture as a sign of the last days. In Paul's last writings, he has warned us as follows:

This know also, that in the last days perilous times shall come. For men shall be lovers of their own selves, covetous, boasters, proud, blasphemers, disobedient to parents, unthankful, unholy; Without natural affection, trucebreakers, false accusers, incontinent, fierce, despisers of those that are good, Traitors, heady, highminded, lovers of pleasures more than lovers of God; Having a form of godliness, but denying the power thereof: from such turn away. For of this sort are they which creep into houses, and lead captive silly women laden with sins, led away with divers lusts, Ever learning, and never able to come to the knowledge of the truth (II Timothy 3:1-7).

This graphic last warning of Paul's perfectly describes the self-centered humanistic behavior of the last days, just as Peter's last warning described the self-centered humanistic philosophy of the last days—the one arising naturally out of the other.

Furthermore, just as the prophetic significance of Peter's prophecy focused especially on the rise of humanistic philosophy in *Christian* nations, so Paul's prophecy notes especially the rise of humanistic behavior in those same Christian nations. In fact, the description here of these humanistic attributes (e.g., self-love, pride, blasphemy, etc.) in those who have a form of religion but no power (that is, those who profess, but do not possess, the genuine experience of saving faith in Christ) is strikingly similar to the description by Paul of the characteristics of the ancient pagans (Romans 1:29-31). That is, one of the key signs of the last days would be the capitulation of Christendom not only to pagan humanistic beliefs but also to pagan humanistic life styles.

This is, indeed, the deplorable situation in the so-called Christian nations of the world today, and it has been growing worse year-by-year. Note just a quick run-down of the listed characteristics, with only a comment or two on each (one could easily document a whole volume of illustrations of each).

1. *"Lovers of their own selves."* Think of the widespread emphasis among Christians today of the importance of a high "self-image," and other self-oriented studies.

2. *"Covetous."* How about the "yuppie generation" and its desire for material goods, an attitude very prevalent even in many evangelical churches with their "prosperity gospel."

3. *"Proud."* This primeval Satanic sin of pride is surely evident today more than ever before, in almost everyone.

4. *"Blasphemers."* The names of God and of Christ are now being taken in vain continuously in literature, the movies, music, television, etc., not to mention the "demythologizing" of the deity that is so common among liberal "Christians."

5. *"Disobedient to parents."* Obedient teen-agers, even in Christian homes, seem to have become an endangered species today, in a society rife with drugs, riotous music, immorality, etc.

6. *"Unthankful."* Affluent American Christians and others rarely thank God for their blessings, and almost totally ignore their role as stewards of these blessings.

7. *"Unholy."* Godlessness and worldliness are more fitting descriptions of people in Christian nations than holiness, a life-style largely ridiculed today.

8. *"Without natural affection."* Witness the sudden rise to respectability and promotion of abortion, and homosexuality, not to mention the increasing prevalence of child abuse and general family violence.

9. *"Trucebreakers."* Treaties between nations, contracts between people, promises in general, are broken at will, and litigation is reaching astronomical heights. The Greek word also means "irreconcilable."

10. *"False accusers."* Defamation, character assassination, libel, slander, as well as everyday malicious gossip, are heard and read everywhere today.

11. *"Incontinent."* Widespread divorce, immorality, promiscuity, marital infidelity and even homosexuality characterize Europe and the Americas today, with even higher statistical frequency than among pagan nations. The term also suggests the widespread addiction to drugs and alcohol.

12. *"Fierce."* The Greek word implies physical brutality, suggesting the modern rise in crime and violence, including especially the murder of millions of unborn children.

13. *"Despisers of those that are good."* What once was considered evil (e.g., homosexuality, pornography) now are considered civil rights, whereas former virtues (e.g., teaching Christian character in school) are now considered dangerous.

14. *"Traitors."* This word applies not only to political treason, of which there is an abundance, but to betrayal of trust in any relationship, of which there are countless instances today, with loyalty almost a forgotten concept even among Christians.

15. *"Heady."* The implication here is carelessness and recklessness, with reference to the rights and feelings of others, doing whatever one pleases with little regard to consequences.

16. *"High-minded."* The same term is elsewhere translated "puffed-up," and refers to personal conceit, a characteristic especially common among both Christian and anti-Christian intellectuals and other people of influence today.

17. *"Lovers of pleasures more than lovers of God."* Just count the number of people in church on any Sunday versus those on pleasure outings, even in our own

"Christian" country, not to mention the abysmal statistics in Europe, Australia and Latin America.

18. *"Having a form of godliness, but denying the power thereof."* Our nation and others may still be called "Christian," but even most mainline churches, as well as the schools, news media, etc., have repudiated creationism and other supernatural aspects of Christianity.

19. *"Ever learning and never able to come to the knowledge of the truth."* This is essentially a definition of modern education, supposedly involved in a perpetual "search for truth" while flatly denying the existence of any absolute or final truth.

While it is true that individuals with these attributes have lived in every age and every place, the combination has never been so universal as now. And the unique aspect is that these now characterize Christian nations as much, if not more, than pagan nations.

The pagan nations of antiquity, like those humanistic cultures in once-Christian nations today, founded their culture on their evolutionary philosophy, "worshiping and serving the creation more than the Creator" (Romans 1:25). This is exactly the situation today, even in once-Christian cultures, and it all surely constitutes a powerful sign that we are in the last days, when "perilous times shall come," because our people have rejected their God.

Social Darwinism, Slavery and War

There are also important sociopolitical and economic-industrial signs of the imminent consummation. We have looked at the last words of Peter and Paul. Now look at those of the Apostle James.

> *Go to now, ye rich men, weep and howl for your miseries which shall come upon you. Your riches are corrupted, and your garments are motheaten.... Ye have heaped treasure together for the last days. Behold, the hire of the laborers, who have reaped down your fields, which is of you kept back by fraud, crieth: ... Ye have lived in pleasure on the earth, and been wanton; ye have nourished your hearts, as in a day of slaughter. Ye have condemned and killed the just; and he doth not resist you. Be patient, therefore, brethren, unto the coming of the Lord. ... stablish your hearts, for the coming of the Lord draweth nigh (James 5:1-8).*

Here is a graphic prophecy of social unrest in the last days. The eternal conflict between rich and poor, capital and labor, master and slave, was evidently going to become more intense than ever in the last days, finally erupting in weeping and howling and miseries and in a great "day of slaughter."

This prophetic sign began to be fulfilled in the Industrial Revolution, which generated great technological advances but also brought great misery to the laboring classes who were exploited mercilessly in the factories and fields of the rich owners—perhaps never more so than in the slave plantations of the Americas. All of this did result in the bloody French Revolution and then later many even more horrible Communist revolutions in Russia, China and other countries, not to mention America's unspeakable Civil War.

While these days of slaughter may to some degree have mitigated the lot of the laboring masses, they also resulted in many cases in even more wealth and power for the great and mighty, as well as ruthless new dictators in many nations. In many cases, in fact, it is known that the revolutions—supposedly of the proletariat against the bourgeoisie—were actually instigated and financed by certain international bankers and leading merchants of Europe and America, with the aim of producing greater riches and power for themselves. These war millionaires actually nourished their hearts in days of slaughter!

Once again, it is noteworthy that wars and slavery, exploitation of labor, capitalistic imperialism and similar practices have been justified by their promulgators on the basis of evolutionism—especially the type of evolutionism promoted since the Industrial Revolution by such cliches as "natural selection," "struggle for existence" and "survival of the fittest."

√ This system came to be known as Social Darwinism, and it was especially promoted in England (by Spencer, Malthus, Darwin and their followers) and in Germany (by Nietzsche, Haeckel, Bismarck, "Kaiser Bill" and eventually Hitler), but also became strong in France (e.g., the Rothschilds) and the United States (through such "robber barons" as John D. Rockefeller, Andrew Carnegie and others). All of these were ardent evolutionists, and perhaps thought their methods were for the long-range good of society, but they resulted in great misery for the masses of people so exploited. The evolutionary background of laissez-faire capitalism, Communism, Nazism, racism, imperialism and the great World Wars is persuasively documented in the book mentioned previously, *The Long War against God*.

In these verses, however, James is telling people not to look to revolutions or legislation for their deliverance, but to "the coming of the Lord," which all these signs foretell. Today, the lot of multitudes of the poor is perhaps worse than ever (think of the poverty-stricken populations in Ethiopia, India, Sudan and many other nations, including those recently escaping from Communist exploitation—perhaps even of the increasing numbers of homeless people and ghetto populations in America), and this sign of the last days becomes more poignant than ever. The real hope, James says, is that "the coming of the Lord draweth nigh."

Apostasy, Rationalism and Occultism

We have noted key latter-day prophecies of the Apostles Peter, Paul and James. These have dealt primarily with worldwide philosophy, morality, and economics, especially, though each had overtones of religious apostasy as well. The other two writers of New Testament epistles also refer to the "last times," in both instances focusing directly on religious issues.

John says: "Little children, it is the last time: and as ye have heard that antichrist shall come, even now are there many antichrists; whereby we know that it is the last time" (I John 2:18).

Jude says: "But, beloved, remember ye the words which were spoken before of the apostles of our Lord Jesus Christ; How that they told you there should be mockers in the last time, who should walk after their own ungodly lusts. These be they who separate themselves, sensual, having not the Spirit" (Jude 17–19).

Thus John warns that the last times will be characterized by "many antichrists" as well as one final "Antichrist," and Jude warns that they will be characterized by unregenerate mocking schismatics. The implication in both cases is that these men will somehow be involved in the church as professing Christians, but will actually be subversives, intending to undermine and destroy the ministry of the church if possible—Satanic plants, as it were.

The original language in John's comment actually says that "we know that it is *a* last hour," rather than *"the* last time." The historical church has gone through many crises, usually brought about by the activities and teachings of unregenerate leaders in their membership, so that it could be said that any such time is "a last time"—that is, a critical hour—for that church or Christian ministry. It must therefore also be true that in *the* last time, there will be many antichrists—that is, not men who claim to be Christ (these are called "false Christs"), but men who seek to oppose the true revealed nature of Christ and His work.

Such men might be *liberals*, seeking to humanize the deity of Christ by eliminating or explaining away those parts of His Word that emphasize His miracles, His Virgin Birth, and His resurrection. On the other hand, they might be *cultists* or *occultists*, seeking to deny His humanity by distinguishing between the man Jesus and the divine Christ, usually by adding to the written Word some new "revelation" supposedly received from the "Christ-spirit of the cosmos," or something of the sort. The one leads to rationalism, ultimately to atheism. The other leads to mysticism, occultism and pantheism. Both types of false teachers must base their apostate, schismatic, notions on some form of evolution—either evolutionary naturalism in the one case, or evolutionary pantheism in the other. Both reject the God of the Bible, the true Creator, Jesus Christ.

Churches are full of such antichrists these days, far more than ever before, and these have, in fact, "caused divisions" (the actual thrust of "separate themselves" in Jude's prophecy) innumerable. John warns against both in the closing verses of his last book as follows:

If any man shall add unto these things, God shall add unto him the plagues that are written in this book. And if any man shall take away from the words of the book of this prophecy, God shall take away his part out of the book of life (Revelation 22:18,19).

In modern times, there has been an explosion—all over the world—of new cults that claim to have new revelation and a new concept of Christ. At the same time, practically all of the traditional denominations (which developed in the past from different interpretations of Scripture, but not from differences regarding Christ or the truth of Scripture) have gone through turmoil and division because of liberals undermining the true divine/human nature of Christ and the inerrant authority of Scripture.

If such things are a sign of the last times—and they are—their proliferation to a degree never seen before in the history of Christianity certainly indicates this sign is being fulfilled today. There are many other Scriptures that forewarn us of this latter-day apostasy, and some will be discussed later, but these suffice to make the point once again that Christ is coming soon.

The Age of Science and Technology

The Old Testament includes many prophetical books, but the book of Daniel contains the most detailed description of the end-times of any book in the Bible, except for the book of Revelation. In Daniel's last chapter, after most of the prophetic portions of his book had been revealed, the mighty angel conveying all these revelations to Daniel closed with the following significant sign by which to recognize the imminence of their fulfillment:

*But thou, O Daniel, shut up the words, and seal
the book, even to the time of the end: many shall
run to and fro, and knowledge shall be increased
(Daniel 12:4).*

Some expositors have taken this to mean that Bible students
in the last days, diligently searching back and forth through
the Scriptures, would finally understand Daniel's prophecies.

The expression "run to and fro," however, is a most
unlikely way to say "search the Scriptures," and "knowledge
shall be increased" is an incomplete way, at best, to say
"understanding of these prophecies will be increased." This
can hardly be the primary meaning of the prediction.

Instead, we are being told that, near the time of the end,
people in large numbers would be "running"—not merely
"traveling," but (literally) "racing"—from one location to
another and back again. At any rate, it is profoundly true
that travel and speed have increased in our times to a degree
that could never have been predicted at all except by supernatural inspiration. In Isaac Newton's day—no less than in
Daniel's day—about the fastest a man could travel would be
on a swift horse. But Newton, who was probably the greatest
scientist of all time, as well as a diligent student and believer
of Daniel's prophecies, claimed on the basis of this verse
that men would someday be able to travel as fast as 50 miles
per hour, even from country to country. A century later,
Voltaire, the French anti-Christian deist, ridiculed this statement, suggesting that Newton's Christianity had affected his
reason.

The fact is that the scientific era which Newton, as much as any one man, introduced, has seen—just in the past century or a little more—invention of the steam locomotive, then the automobile, then the airplane, now the space-ship hurtling through space at incredible speeds. This prophecy could hardly have been fulfilled more explicitly than it is now being fulfilled in this "time of the end."

The other half of the prophecy—"knowledge shall be increased"—could well be translated *"science* shall be increased," for the two words are synonymous in meaning and derivation. The scientific and technological advances in just the past generation are legion—radio, television, electrical appliances to do almost everything, super-highways, nuclear power, computers, automation, radar, plastics, microchips, robots, and on and on. Less than two centuries ago, all the scientists in the world probably could have convened in one large auditorium; now there are millions of them, working in hundreds of scientific disciplines. Not surprisingly, the founding fathers of our scientific age—men such as Newton, Kepler, Boyle, Pasteur, Pascal, Faraday, Joule, Galileo, Euler, Maxwell, etc.—were almost all Christian creationists. On the other hand, the study of evolution—whether in astronomy, biology, anthropology, or any other field—has contributed nothing whatever to these scientific discoveries and technological inventions that have so advanced human longevity, productivity and standards of living. It is noteworthy that explosive advances in both true science and the numbers of scientists committed in their philosophy (if not in their practice!) to false science are both given in Scripture as signs of the last days.

Once again we marvel at the prophetic insights of the writers of the prophetic Scriptures of the end times, each stressing a particular worldwide sign of the end near the very close of his own contribution to the canon of Scripture. Note, in review:

(1) Daniel noted the great advances in science and rapid travel and communications near the time of the end.

(2) Peter stressed the worldwide dominance of a naturalistic philosophy of evolutionary humanism in the last days.

(3) Paul foresaw the universal moral and spiritual decay of the last days, with the rise of humanistic behavior based on the world's humanistic philosophy.

(4) James predicted global industrial and economic conflicts in the last days, leading to great wars and revolutions.

(5) John and Jude both emphasized the great religious apostasy of the last time, with both atheism and pantheism diluting true Christianity.

Finally we come to the great prophecy given by Christ Himself, as recorded by Matthew, Mark and Luke in the closing pages of *their* writings. Except for His intimate teachings to the disciples the night before His arrest and crucifixion, this "Olivet Discourse" was His final formal message, and it does incorporate many signs of His second coming.

The Great Sign Given by Christ

Just before His crucifixion, the disciples asked Christ: "Tell us, when shall these things be? And what shall be the sign of thy coming, and of the end of the world?" (Matthew 24:3).

He had been talking to them about the coming destruction of Jerusalem and the temple, and also had told them several times about His coming substitutionary death and resurrection. They were unable to fit all this together, especially when they had also been thinking in the past that, as their promised Messiah, He would soon expel their Roman rulers and set up His own kingdom in Jerusalem. Hence their question. His answer is given in part in Matthew 24, part in Mark 13, part in Luke 21. There is much overlap, but also each writer includes a portion not found in the other two. Thus one should study the three accounts simultaneously to get the complete answer to the disciples' questions. There were actually three questions: (1) When will the temple be destroyed? (2) What is the sign of Christ's return? (3) When will the end of the world (or "end of the age") occur?

First, the Lord indicated that certain events which might be taken as signs really were *not* signs, but normal occurrences throughout history prior to the end:

> *Take heed that ye be not deceived: for many shall come in my name, saying I am Christ; and the*

time draweth near: go ye not therefore after
them. But when ye shall hear of wars and com-
motions [Matthew and Mark say "rumors of
wars" here], be not terrified: for these things
must first come to pass; but the end is not by
and by (Luke 21:8,9).

There have, indeed, been many pseudo-Christs and wars
and rumors of wars and various types of commotions all
through the centuries since His ascension, so this particular
prophecy has been explicitly fulfilled, thus increasing our
confidence that the rest will be fulfilled as well.

Then Christ paused before continuing, indicating that He
was now about to answer their specific questions.

Then said He unto them, Nation shall rise
against nation, and kingdom against kingdom:
And great earthquakes shall be in divers places,
and famines, and pestilences [Mark says "and
troubles"]; and fearful sights and great signs
shall there be from heaven (Luke 21:10–11).

In other words, the sign of His coming, as requested by
the disciples, would be a multi-faceted sign. The first component would be a great multi-national war, not just a
two-sided war. At least two nations and two kingdoms would
be fighting; actually the expression is an idiom denoting a
general war involving many nations, especially the world's
major nations.

Then, following that, there would be great earthquakes, famines, pestilences and troubles in various places around the world, as well as fearful sights in the heavens. This combined sign is evidently the sign the disciples requested. Since the parallel passages (Matthew 24 and Mark 13) do not mention signs in the heavens at this point, the reference in Luke probably applies only to the later stages of the great sign.

There have been many, many wars since Christ spoke these words, as well as many earthquakes, famines, plagues and other calamities. But the first time a great multi-national war occurred was the first World War, in 1914–18. And this war was, indeed, followed by tremendous earthquakes in China, Japan and other places, as well as tremendous famines in China, Russia and other nations, along with what was probably the deadliest plague of history, the great influenza epidemic of 1918. It does seem possible—even probable— that this was truly the asked-for sign of His approaching return.

But then Jesus said this was merely the "beginning of travail," comparing the coming of His kingdom to the birth of a child. There must be a number of similar labor pains, occurring at intervals, before the sign would be complete. World War One was only the *first* birth pain.

It was soon followed by others, however. Beginning with Japan's invasion of China, then Mussolini's invasion of Ethiopia, and Hitler's *Blitzkrieg* into Poland in 1939, soon the whole world was at war again. The end of World War II in 1945 was then followed by the establishment of the United Nations, which the nations all hoped would prevent future wars.

It did not, of course. Soon came the Korean "conflict," then after that the Indo-China wars, culminating in the Viet Nam disaster. These wars also involved many nations. Very recently, (1990–1991), the world witnessed practically the entire United Nations Organization at war against Iraq, followed by still futher turmoil in the Middle East, all affecting nations in all parts of the world.

Along with these multi-national wars there have been scores of local wars in every part of the world, as well as "terrible famines, and pestilences and earthquakes in divers places" scattered throughout the 70+ years since the first birth pang. It may not be clear yet how many more are still to come, but we surely must be nearing the end. The "fearful sights from heaven" possibly involve the supposed UFO phenomena during this period, or the variety of spacecraft that have been launched into the heavens. More likely, the great signs in the heavens are still to come in the near future.

Following the giving of this first great "sign of His coming and of the end of the [age]," Jesus then turned his prophecy back again to the general characteristics of the immediate apostolic period. But before all these, "He said, they shall lay their hands on you, and persecute you, ..." (Luke 21:12). This initial wave of persecution was to continue until the destruction of Jerusalem and the dispersion of the Jews. "They shall fall by the edge of the sword, and shall be led away captive into all nations: and Jerusalem shall be trodden down of the Gentiles, ..." (Luke 21:24). This portion of His prophecy will be discussed in Chapter 3. It was specifically fulfilled in 70 A.D., when the Roman general (later emperor) Titus did, indeed, destroy the temple; then, later, Hadrian's armies destroyed the city itself, sending the Jews off in 135 A.D. into their 1800-year dispersion among the nations.

There are still other significant signs in this key prophetic message of Christ, also known as the Olivet Discourse, but these will be discussed later.

CHAPTER 2

Turmoil in the Bible Lands

Religious Background of the Middle East

There are many nations of the world whose dominant religions consist of some form of evolutionary pantheism. These include Hinduism, Buddhism, Confucianism, Taoism, Shintoism and Animism. In each of these pantheistic nations, there are pockets of Christians, Jews and Muslims, of course, as well as atheists, but most of the people are polytheistic pantheists. All of these religious systems deny the existence of a personal, transcendent Creator God, assuming instead the eternal pre-existence of matter and the space-time universe. Thus, all of them are basically evolutionist religions. Like the pagans of Greece, Rome and the other nations of antiquity, they have "changed the truth of God into a lie, and worshiped and served the creature more than the Creator" (Romans 1:25).

There are three religions in the world, however, that are basically monotheistic, believing in a real Creator and in the creation of the universe by the Word of God. One of these, Judaism, is now centered officially in Israel, although Jews are found in every nation. Christianity is nominally the religion of Europe, the Americas, Australia, New Zealand and South Africa. Islam is the religion of the Middle East especially, as well as much of North and East Africa, Indonesia and parts of central Asia.

It is interesting and perhaps prophetically significant that the present turmoil in the Middle East primarily seems to involve monotheistic nations battling each other, while the great pantheistic nations, with their religions composed of a potent mixture of mysticism, occultism and atheism, are mostly just standing by, infiltrating other religions wherever possible but otherwise aloof from the immediate conflicts. It is significant also that the turmoil is all situated in the lands of the Bible, causing many once again to look to the Scriptures for understanding.

The Middle and Near Eastern nations (except for Israel and a Christian minority in Lebanon) are today all Moslem nations. Despite the similarities of Islam to Judaism and Christianity, the religious leaders of Islam seem to hate both Jews and Christians with deep ferocity, and the resultant turmoil in these nations, under their religious militant fanaticism, will inevitably grow worse.

There are 18 Moslem nations in this region, as follows; Afghanistan, Bahrain, Egypt, Iran, Iraq, Jordan, Kuwait,

Lebanon, Libya, Oman, Pakistan, Qatar, Saudi Arabia, Syria, Turkey, United Arab Emirates, North Yemen and South Yemen. The Palestinian settlements in Israel, with their Palestinian Liberation Organization, aspire to nationhood also, but Israel has strongly resisted this so far (as of 1991). The Kurds (of Turkey, Iran and Iraq) also seek an autonomous status, as do other ethnic and religious groups. Several of the "republics" in the currently disintegrating "Union of Soviet Socialist Republics" are largely Muslim in ethnic background.

The Recent War with Iraq

In addition to hating Israel, these Muslim nations often quarrel among themselves (note especially the bitter eight-year war between Iran and Iraq). Hardly had their war with Iran ended (essentially in stalemate), before Iraq then invaded and pillaged its small Muslim neighbor Kuwait. Islamic nations became—for a while at least—seriously divided. Egypt, Saudi Arabia, Syria and the smaller Arab states on the Persian Gulf joined up with the United States and most of Europe to fight Iraq, Jordan, South Yemen, Sudan and Libya aligned themselves with Iraq, while most of the others tried to remain somewhat neutral. Israel also tried to remain neutral, although Iraq tried from the very first, by wanton missile attacks, to force Israel to fight, confident that all the Muslim nations would then side with her against Israel and its friends. Surprisingly, even though she could have destroyed Iraq with nuclear bombs, Israel showed great restraint in refusing to retaliate against Iraq.

In initiating his conflict with Iran and then with the United Nations, Iraq's murderous dictator, Saddam Hussein, seemed to envision himself as eventually becoming the leader of the entire Moslem world. Herein lies much of the prophetic significance of the current Mid-East turmoil. Many even suggested that Saddam might be the prophesied Antichrist, but this was evidently wrong.

Iraq was the strongest and wealthiest of all the Mid-East Muslim nations, and is an extremely significant nation in Biblical prophecy. The Arab nations as a whole control 65% of the world's oil supply, and Iraq had made herself the strongest of them all, as well as the most strategically located.

✓ Baghdad, the capital of Iraq, is situated very close to the ruins of ancient Babylon, once the greatest city in the world and, in the days of Nebuchadnezzar, the capital of the most powerful nation in the world. Saddam Hussein considered himself the second Nebuchadnezzar, destined to rule the world once again from Babylon. With this dream in view, he diligently began the enormous task of rebuilding and restoring Babylon to its former glory. Such a project (actually begun by Iraq in 1971) would have been inconceivable 20 years earlier, when oil first began to be produced in quantity in the Middle East, but Iraq's huge oil revenues and Soviet ties had almost made it a reality by the time of Saddam's Kuwait invasion. Whether Saddam was aware that he was thereby fulfilling Biblical prophecy is unknown, but the Bible does indicate that Babylon will once again become a great world capital (see Chapter 4).

Saddam, however, will not be the one who reigns there! He does not at all fit the Biblical description of the coming Antichrist (see Chapter 5). He is merely another in a long line of ambitious "antichrists" (e.g., Napoleon, Mussolini, Hitler, Stalin, Mao-tse-tung, etc.) who aspired to world dominion, but ended up in a tomb.

Iraq's great oil wealth also enabled Saddam to erect a mighty military arsenal, purchasing advanced and deadly weaponry from the Soviet Union and other European nations, with Soviet technicians provided in abundance for the necessary instruction and implementation. Unfortunately, the United States also invested heavily in Iraq's military machine, "tilting" toward Iraq in the Iran-Iraq War because of Iran's anti-American stance under the Ayatollah Khomeini, following her rebellion against the former Shah, America's ally.

The deadly war following Saddam's intransigent refusal to abandon Kuwait, even after condemnation by the United Nations, has subjected Iraq to such a degree of devastation that it may be impossible for Iraq ever to regain Arab leadership again.

But there are other Middle East nations that are also ambitious and perhaps able, to fill the vacuum left by Iraq's defeat—such nations as Iran or Syria, or perhaps Turkey or Libya. Egypt once had such ambitions, but was badly defeated by Israel in 1967, and the Bible says Egypt will always remain "the basest among nations" (Ezekiel 29:15). The present government in Turkey is friendly to the United States, but there is a strong undercurrent of Marxist sentiment there, and also of Moslem fundamentalism, and this could easily change. All of these countries have very large standing armies and are heavily armed with weaponry, mostly from the West.

More ominous than any of these, however, was the Soviet Union itself. It has had actual treaties with Iraq, as well as Syria, South Yemen, Libya, and others, as well as great influence with most of the other Moslem countries of the Middle East. Although the Soviet "Union" is changing, historical and economic consideration assure that its various republics must continue in some kind of alliance, with dominant influence still in Russia itself.

In fact, the Soviet Union could almost have been considered another Mid-East Muslim nation itself, for many of its "republics" are themselves almost entirely Muslim. These are Azerbaijan, Kazakhistan, Kirgizia, Tajikistan, Turkmenistan, and Uzbekistan. Large pockets of Muslims dominate many other regions of the Soviet Union as well. Indeed, it is estimated that at least 18% (some have claimed up to 40%) of the U.S.S.R. population consists of ethnic Muslims, though many of these may actually be atheists.

A very significant aspect of this situation is that the Soviet army has an abnormally large percentage of Muslims, including especially many of its more influential generals. It is well known that most of Russia's army generals have opposed the recent *glasnost* reforms in Soviet society, and have insisted that Russia retain its great military strength, despite superficial reductions negotiated in various disarmament agreements. Although, for economic reasons, the Soviet military has gone along with the break-up of Russia's satellite empire, it adamantly refused to endorse the disintegration of the Soviet Union itself. Gorbachev had to yield to this pressure and, despite the shambles and shortages of its economy, Russia still retains its global superiority in both nuclear and conventional arms.

Thankfully, its interlude of "openness"—no doubt allowed mainly to acquire urgently needed American economic and technological assistance—has resulted in a tremendous influx of Christian witness into both Russia and her former satellites in eastern Europe. Great numbers of Bibles and Christian books, as well as evangelists and Bible teachers, have been eagerly received into this atheist nation.

There has even been a significant turning to creationism among Russian scientists, and many who have come to saving faith in Christ.

Unfortunately, this situation will not last, for Biblical prophecy indicates otherwise. We are thankful for all who can be reached for the Lord while the Russian door remains open, but sooner or later the anti-Christians in the Soviet Union—the Moslem and other reactionary generals in the army, the former KGB leaders and the hard-core Communists in the Politburo, the atheistic intellectuals among the scientists and educators, the strong and growing contingent of occultic and "New Age" adherents and others—will regain control and continue their ruthless drive toward world hegemony.

The *glasnost* interlude has served a number of purposes for this evil conspiracy. Russia has divested herself of the economic drag of her satellites in Eastern Europe and inveigled a great deal of economic aid from the United States, all of which has enabled her to keep her military machine at full strength. She has also been able to keep on good terms with the many Muslim nations, both those that fought Iraq (through overt cooperation with the United Nations) and those that supported Iraq (through covert aid to Iraq). Finally, all those Russians who have shown openness to the Gospel will have thereby exposed themselves as "unreliables," for the benefit of future purges.

At the time of this writing (September, 1991), the war with Iraq, supported by the United Nations but fought largely by the United States, is barely over, and the chaotic changes in the Soviet Union are still going on, so I certainly cannot be dogmatic about these analyses and forecasts of future developments. Prophecy is easier to explain after it has been fulfilled than before. Nevertheless, the Lord has given us some rather explicit information concerning these latter-day events, and He does expect us to seek to understand them and to be guided by them as they begin to happen. Some of the most important and explicit Biblical prophecies do, indeed, refer to the role of Russia, Israel and these Middle Eastern nations in the last days, and current developments seem to be moving rapidly toward these future events described so graphically in the Bible.

Moslems against Israel

One of the strange phenomena of our times is the bitter hatred of all Moslems toward Israel and her religion. Both religions believe in a transcendent God of creation and in His revelation in Genesis, but both groups regard themselves as God's chosen people descended from Abraham—Israel through Isaac, as recorded through Moses and David, and the Moslems through Ishmael as revealed by the prophet Mohammed. To the Moslems—both Arabic and non-Arabic—God is Allah, the distant but omnipotent God of might and judgment. To the Israelites, God is especially revealed in His redemptive, loving character as Jehovah, or Yahweh.

The Bible, of course, had been completed long before the rise of Mohammed and the Moslem religion around 600 AD. Nevertheless, it often refers to the Mid-East peoples who would eventually comprise the Moslem world, and frequently indicates their inveterate hatred of Israel. Often these sections are ultimately prophetic in character. One of the most important of these is the 83rd Psalm.

Psalm 83 was written by Asaph, David's musician, but the prophesied event it describes did not take place in David's time at all. Some commentators have seen its later fulfillment in Jehoshophat's reign, some in Jeremiah's time, some in the time of the Macabees. None of these really fit, however, and it seems that it actually must refer to the end-times when, finally, "men may know that thou, whose name alone is JEHOVAH, art the Most High over all the earth" (Psalm 83:18).

In his prophetic vision, Asaph sees surrounding Israel a confederacy of nations whose sole purpose is to destroy Israel. "They have said, Come, and let us cut them off from being a nation; that the name of Israel may be no more in remembrance" (Psalm 83:4).

This league of ten nations includes the following: "Edom, and the Ishmaelites; of Moab, and the Hagarenes; Gebal, and Ammon, and Amalek; the Philistines with the inhabitants of Tyre; Assur also is joined with them" (Psalm 83:6-8). Asaph, of course, describes this anti-Israel confederacy in terms of then-existing nations, but since the prophecy is really for the end-times, we must translate these names into their modern geographic equivalents, the most significant point being that they were the nations immediately surrounding Israel as it existed in the time of King David—long before Persia, Babylon or even Assyria had become great powers in more distant regions. On the east were Edom, Ammon and Moab (in what is now Jordan). Southeast were the Ishmaelites and Hagarenes. Southwest were the Amalekites. These are now partly in Jordan, partly in Saudi Arabia. Directly west on the seacoast were the Philistines, now the Palestinians. On the north were the Phoenician city-states, Tyre and Gebal—the area known now as Lebanon, more recently largely annexed by Syria. Northeast was Assur, the beginnings of what would soon become the great Assyrian empire. This area is now partly Syria, partly Iraq.

Over the centuries, there has been a great commingling of these and other Middle Eastern peoples, so it is no longer possible to make a one-to-one identification among these ancient nations and their modern counterparts. The point is that Israel's ancient enemies are the direct ancestors of her modern enemies, even though the subsequent mix of national identities has been profound.

In any case, Asaph foresaw a time when all the nations immediately surrounding Israel would resolve to destroy Israel and remove her completely from her God-given lands, and this is exactly the situation today. It is remarkable that the modern state of Israel, small as it is, has prevailed in one war after another with its Arab neighbors—Jordan, Egypt, Syria, Palestine, Iraq, etc. Nevertheless, with these and all the other Moslem nations becoming stronger all the time—with arms from Russia, Germany, France, China and even the United States—it would seem impossible for Israel to win a deadly war with the entire Moslem world, especially if supported by Russia. This is exactly what seems to be on the horizon, however—except for God!

Just as God intervened long ago at the Red Sea with miraculous power to save Israel—as He also did against the Midianites in the days of Gideon and the Canaanites in the days of Deborah (note Psalm 83:9-12)—so He will in these last days. There will be a great storm of wind (verses 13,15) and a great fire on the mountains (verse 14), which will leave these Moslem armies "confounded and troubled for ever" (verse 17). Then those who remain will finally acknowledge that JEHOVAH—not Allah—is "the Most High over all the earth" (verse 18).

Gog and Magog

The same future conflict seems to be in view in a prophecy given some 400 years later, though indicating a much broader scope of the confederacy arrayed against Israel. This prophecy was given through the prophet Ezekiel, one of the Jewish priests taken captive to Babylon by Nebuchadnezzar, and is the famous "Gog-and-Magog" prophecy (Ezekiel 38-39).

In Chapter 37, immediately preceding, Ezekiel had predicted a future return of the Jews to the land of Israel. This prediction, however, did not refer to the first return under Ezra and Nehemiah, but to a future return under "an everlasting covenant," with God's "sanctuary in the midst of them forevermore" (Ezekiel 37:26). After almost 2000 years of exile following their rejection of Christ, the Jews did begin to return again under the Balfour Declaration and the Zionist movement, beginning in World War I when the British liberated Jerusalem from the Turks and proposed to establish a Jewish homeland there. Then, in 1948, after World War II, Israel was recognized by the United Nations Organization as a sovereign state, and has functioned as an independent nation ever since, despite all the efforts of her Moslem enemies to cast her out into the sea.

However, Israel has not yet acknowledged Jesus Christ as her long-awaited Messiah; in fact, a large segment of the nation is essentially either atheistic or pantheistic, firmly committed to the evolutionary view of human history rather than the Biblical record—even the record of their own early history. The people of Israel have now reached the stage of Ezekiel's prophecy where they were to have been raised out of their graves among the nations and brought back to Israel, but with no real life in them (note Ezekiel 37:8,13).

This is the setting of Ezekiel 38, describing a future time when a great confederacy of nations decides to invade and despoil "the land that is brought back from the sword, and is gathered out of many people, against the mountains of Israel, which have been always waste; but it is brought forth out of the nations" (Ezekiel 38:8). The time of this invasion "shall be in the latter days" (Ezekiel 38:16), and thus applies specifically not to the times of Ezekiel, or even of the apostles, but to the end-times.

The makeup of the confederacy is interesting and important. The leader is a man named "Gog" of the "land of Magog" (Ezekiel 38:2). He is thrice identified as "the chief prince of Meshech and Tubal" (Ezekiel 38:2,3; 39:1). However, the words "chief prince" could be translated as "prince of Rosh," (and are so rendered in many modern translations) and there is considerable evidence that it was understood this way by the early Greek church and its descendants, including the Russian Orthodox Church. These sources suggest, in fact, that the very name "Russia" was derived originally by the early people of Russia (known then as "Rus") from this Scripture. If so, this passage strongly suggests that Gog is the head of Russia in these latter times.

This etymological derivation (of Russia from Rosh) is not certain, but even without it, the Russian connection is indicated by the association of Gog with Meshech and Tubal, as well as Magog. These three were originally sons of Japheth, the son of Noah. The few cryptic references in the Bible to the tribes descended from these men seem to indicate only that they lived in distant lands and were people of cruelty. However, Assyrian inscriptions, as well as references to them in the histories of Herodotus and Josephus, indicate that they lived in various areas well north of Israel in Old Testament times, later migrating still further north. Many scholars believe that descendants of theirs founded the cities of Moscow and Tobolsk—in west and east Russia, respectively—thus preserving their tribal names even into the present day.

Associated with their Russian leader in the invasion of Israel will be "Persia, Ethiopia, and Libya"...; Gomer, and all his bands, the house of Togarmah of the north quarters, and all his bands: and many people with thee" (Ezekiel 38:5,6). Persia, Ethiopia and Libya are well known in the modern world, but this reference may include more than is implied by just the nations of today.

In Ezekiel's time, Persia included much of modern Iraq as well as Iran. Ethiopia probably included much of the Sudan and possibly Somalia and (just across the Red Sea) Yemen.

Libya was essentially the same then as now, but may also have included areas of northern Africa now west of Libya and possibly even portions of southern Egypt. Both Ethiopia (Cush in the Hebrew) and Libya (Phut in Hebrew), as well as Egypt (Mizraim) and Canaan, were children of Ham, Noah's rebellious son (Genesis 10:6). Again, however, their descendants in modern times represent millennia of national mixing and interbreeding.

Gomer was another son of Japheth (Genesis 10:2), brother to Magog, Meshech and Tubal. His descendants settled in northern Asia Minor, north of the Black Sea (the name being preserved by the Cimmerians), and possibly also in the Crimea. They were probably still there in Ezekiel's day, although they were later driven out by the Lydians. Some scholars believe they eventually moved west, with their name finally preserved as Germany. In Ezekiel's prophecy, the name probably refers to the area of modern Turkey. The phrase "all his bands" may refer to tribes descended from Gomer's sons—Ashhenaz (referring probably to the Scythians, who lived in Asia Minor and southern Russia, or even to Germany, as believed by the German Jews of medieval times, who called themselves Ashkenazi), and Riphath (identified by Josephus with the Paphlagonians, who also lived in Asia Minor but later migrated into Russia).

"Togarmah of the north quarters" was the third son of Gomer, but is listed separately by Ezekiel, evidently because of his importance. He is commonly believed to be the ancestor of the Armenians, a very ancient nation with roots in Turkey (around Mount Ararat), and now a "republic" of the U.S.S.R. It is also possible that modern Turkomen, another U.S.S.R. republic near Armenia, could be derived from Togarmah. The names Turkestan and even Turkey could have a similar origin.

Gog, the human leader of this invading confederacy, is a man's name, of course, but it is also possibly related to the U.S.S.R. republic of Georgia, adjacent to both Turkey and Armenia. In Russia, the name "George" would be pronounced "Gyorg" with a hard "g," sounding essentially like "Gog." It is interesting that the first Russian premier following the death of Stalin had this name (Georgi Malenkov), and many Russian political leaders have come from Georgia. Malenkov, during his brief rule, was largely responsible for giving the Moslems greater influence in the U.S.S.R.

Although the names cannot be identified with modern equivalents with certainty, there is a strong case that all relate either to modern Russia or to the Moslem nations on the periphery of those Moslem nations immediately surrounding Israel. The names, in fact, seem to proceed clockwise around Israel. Beginning with Iran/Iraq in the east, then Ethiopia/Sudan in the south, Libya in the west, Turkey in the northwest, Armenia/Turkestan in the northeast—all are overseen by Russia coming from the far north. In addition, there are other unnamed nations—"many people with thee" (verse 6).

As seen from Psalm 83, the nations on the immediate perimeter of Israel (Jordan, northern Arabia, Palestine, Lebanon, Syria) are also involved, so the whole array seems extremely formidable. And these are the hordes which will suddenly invade tiny Israel! But God says: "I am against thee, O Gog" (Ezekiel 38:3), and they are merely pressing toward their own destruction!

The Burial of Gog

In describing the invasion, Ezekiel necessarily has to use a vocabulary meaningful to the people of his day (actually also quite applicable to all periods of history except the modern period). Ezekiel and his readers knew nothing of tanks and artillery and airplanes, and so had to speak of horses, swords and storm clouds to convey what he saw in his vision. He wrote of "horses and horsemen, clothed with all sorts of armor, a great company with bucklers and shields, all of them handling swords," also of "a great company, and a mighty army," and of ascending "like a storm, ... like a cloud to cover the land" (verse 4,15,9, etc.). This speaks of a tremendous strike force by both land and air, a *blitzkrieg*, as Hitler would have called it.

There are a few nations that will object to this surprise attack. "Sheba and Dedan, and the merchants of Tarshish, with all the young lions thereof, shall say unto (Gog), Art thou come to take a spoil? Hast thou gathered thy company to take a prey?" (Ezekiel 38:13). The objection is only verbal, however, rather than aggressive. The attack is too sudden for them to stop it. As seen in the Iraqi invasion of Kuwait, it took months for the U.N. coalition to stage an effective fighting force to liberate the invaded nation.

The identity of the remonstrating nations (Sheba, Dedan, Tarshish) is uncertain in terms of modern equivalents, but it will be likely those nations that have previously opposed a Russian or Moslem takeover in the region. Sheba and Dedan are clearly somewhere in Arabia, and most likely represent the rich nations of the Persian Gulf (Saudi Arabia, Kuwait, Qatar, Oman, United Arab Emirates), whose fabulous wealth of energy resources is probably the ultimate object of Russian and Moslem cupidity, in addition to the chemical and technological wealth of Israel. It is noteworthy that neither Egypt nor Assyria (northern Iraq) nor most of Saudi Arabia seem to be included in this confederacy.

The merchants of Tarshish most likely represent a latter-day version of the ancient sea-faring Phoenicians, who had been made wealthy by their merchant marine, sailing from their colonial ports in Carthage (possibly etymologically derived from "Tarshish"), Spain and Britain, in addition to their great home bases in Tyre and Sidon. In later times, both Spain and England continued this sea-faring tradition, both with great fleets and extensive colonies in the Americas. "The young lions thereof" would presumably refer to these colonies. Today this mantle seems to rest primarily on Great Britain and the "British lion," plus her "young lions," namely Canada, Australia and the United States. In the current context, it would not be surprising at all that the main objections to the Russian/Moslem invasion would come from the United States, England and the wealthy Arab states of the Persian Gulf (the latter not because of concern for Israel, but because of the very realistic fear that they would be next).

Note that the attack will come by surprise. Not only are the objecting nations unprepared, but Israel will have become "the land of unwalled villages," and the people who are "at rest, that dwell safely, ... having neither bars nor gates" (Ezekiel 38:11).

This certainly does not fit the case right now with all of Israel's Moslem neighbors threatening her very existence. From this fact, we have to conclude that the recent war with Iraq was not the direct prelude to the Russian/Moslem invasion prophesied here in Ezekiel 38.

Before that invasion begins, therefore, there must first be at least one brief period of calm and assumed safety. There must be a cessation of the fighting while Israel takes a welcome rest, America and England relax their guards and bring most of their troops home, and Russia acquires effective leadership over all the Moslem nations around Israel (except Egypt and Arabia). Presumably, then will come the surprise attack against Israel, one that neither Israel nor her friends are prepared to resist.

Right here is when God will intervene, however, just as already suggested in Psalm 83. "Surely in that day there shall be a great shaking in the land of Israel; ... and the mountains shall be thrown down, ... every man's sword will be against his brother. And I will plead against him with pestilence and with blood; and I will rain upon him, and upon his bands, and upon the many people that are with him, an overflowing rain, and great hailstones, fire and brimstone." (Ezekiel 38:19-22).

Only one-sixth of the invading hordes will survive this terrible holocaust (Ezekiel 39:2), and it will take seven months for "men of continual employment" to "bury Gog and all his multitude" (verses 14,11) there in the land of Israel.

Furthermore it will take seven years (verse 9) to burn all the flammable portions of the planes, tanks, ammunition and other military materials left by Gog's armies. It is at least a possibility that this will be the same seven-year period set by God for His imminent judgment on all the ungodly nations of the world, the great coming "tribulation" period.

After this great deliverance, there will be no more atheism or New-Age pantheism in Israel. "The house of Israel shall know that I am the LORD, the Holy One in Israel" (verse 7). Both Jew and Gentile will know henceforth that there is a God in heaven who claims to be the Creator and Judge of all men.

But amazingly enough, this does not mean that they will also accept Him as Savior and Lord! So this is not yet the happy ending of the story, by any means.

CHAPTER 3

The Amazing Renaissance of Israel

A Miracle Nation

The nation of Israel is truly a unique phenomenon among the nations of the world. It began almost 4,000 years ago with the family of Jacob (or Israel) and his twelve sons. Most of the contemporary nations at the time—the Elamites, the Chaldeans, the Hittites, the Perizzites, the Amorites, the Philistines, the Horites, and others—have long been extinct as nations, but Israel is alive and well and is, in fact, the very hub of international concern. The boiling Middle East, as discussed in the preceding chapter, can be understood only in terms of the role of Israel in the Middle East.

Furthermore, among the signs of the imminent return of Christ, as delineated in Chapter 1, the very existence of Israel, and especially her return to her homeland and her restoration as a sovereign nation surely constitutes the most persuasive sign of all. In subjection to foreign rulers for 2,500 years, without even a national home for over 1,800 years, then suddenly back from the grave, as it were—nothing like this has ever happened elsewhere in all history. Yet it was all predicted in the Bible to happen just this way! Israel is not only a compelling proof of Biblical inerrancy, it is a sure witness that the second coming of Christ is very near.

The call of Israel as God's chosen nation was the fulfillment of His unconditional promise to faithful Abraham.

> *Get thee out of thy country, and from thy kindred, and from thy father's house, into a land that I will show thee: And I will make of thee a great nation, and I will bless thee, and make thy name great; and thou shalt be a blessing: And I will bless them that bless thee, and curse him that curseth thee: and in thee shall all families of the earth be blessed (Genesis 12:1-3).*

This prophetic promise, made 4000 years ago, has been fulfilled again and again in world history. The nations that have befriended the children of Israel (e.g., United States) have been greatly blessed. Those that have persecuted Israel (Assyria, Babylonia, Imperial Rome, Nazi Germany, etc.) have eventually disintegrated under God's curse.

Before God called Israel, the other nations had all rebelled against His Word. He had cleansed the antediluvian world with the great flood, but it took only three generations before the descendants of Noah also rebelled against Him, at Babel. There Nimrod, Noah's great grandson, led the people into the God-denying religion of evolutionary pantheism that has dominated human thought ever since, and God had to confuse their languages and separate the nations.

God then established a special nation through which to reveal His Word and bring the promised Savior into the world. Because of Abraham's strong faith and obedience, God chose him to begin the new nation, and then made an unconditional and very specific promise concerning the territory of this nation.

Unto thy seed have I given this land, from the river of Egypt unto the great river, the river Euphrates (Genesis 15:18).

All the land then occupied by the many Canaanite tribes, as well as others, all the way from the Nile to the Euphrates, was to be the land of Israel. This apparently has been attained only for a brief period under David and Solomon. Even though this was only a temporary fulfillment of the promise, it eventually will be permanently fulfilled.

But it has been a long time coming. God promised great blessing to Israel as long as its people were faithful, but judgment and exile if they turned away.

But it shall come to pass, if thou wilt not hearken unto the voice of the LORD thy God, to observe to do all His commandments and His statutes which I command thee this day; that all these curses shall come upon thee, and overtake thee: ... And the LORD shall scatter thee among all

people, from the one end of the earth even unto
the other: and there thou shalt serve other gods,
which neither thou nor thy fathers have known,
even wood and stone. And among these nations
shalt thou find no ease, neither shall the sole of
thy foot have rest: but the LORD shall give thee
there a trembling heart, and failing of eyes, and
sorrow of mind (Deuteronomy 28:15; 64-65).

This and many similar prophecies were all fulfilled explicitly in the long, long exile of the "wandering Jew."
Through the centuries, for 1800 years, in almost every
country, the Israelites have been hated and ridiculed and
persecuted. Unlike other captive or exiled peoples, however,
they were never either eliminated or assimilated by the
people around them, always retaining their distinct identity
and continuing to look for their promised Messiah, refusing
to acknowledge that He had already come and been rejected
by them.

And thou shalt become an astonishment, a
proverb, and a byword, among all nations
whither the LORD shall lead thee (Deuteronomy
28:37).

Lo, the people shall dwell alone, and shall not
be reckoned among the nations (Numbers 23:9).

Over the centuries, the land of Israel grew more and more
desolate, though still supporting a small population of Arabs,
Maronite Christians and a remnant of Jews. The city of
Jerusalem itself, although devastated by the Romans in 135

A.D., was later revived in measure as a religious site. At various times it has been controlled by Romans, Syrians, Arabs, Crusaders, Egyptians, Persians and Turks, then finally by the British, but never again by the Jews, until our own generation.

The Jews have been persecuted all over the world and all through the centuries, yet have survived. Furthermore, they have produced far more than their proportionate share of leaders—in science, business, education, medicine, law, and other fields requiring both ability and industry. They have continued to maintain not only their national identity, but their religion, and their Messianic hope for the future. Israel has, indeed, been a miracle nation, confirming God's Word, to persevere as they have through the centuries. An even greater miracle, however, has been their amazing revival as a sovereign nation in the modern world.

Promises of Restoration

Few people realize—even among Christians—how many and how definite are God's promises to restore Israel in the last days. Even before they had entered the land of Canaan to begin their divinely promised conquest, God had both warned the children of Israel of exile from the land if they rebelled (as noted in the foregoing section), and promised their eventual return.

And yet for all that, when they be in the land of their enemies, I will not cast them away, neither will I abhor them, to destroy them utterly, and

> *to break my covenant with them: for I am the*
> *LORD their God (Leviticus 26:44).*

God does not break His covenant, for He is the eternal
God.

> *Then will I remember my covenant with Jacob,*
> *and also my covenant with Isaac, and also my*
> *covenant with Abraham will I remember; and I*
> *will remember the land (Leviticus 26:42).*

Arabs and others may dispute the ownership of the land,
but the land of Israel is God's land, for He created it, and
He promised it to the descendants of Abraham, Isaac and
Jacob.

> *God is not a man, that He should lie; neither*
> *the son of man, that He should repent; hath He*
> *said, and shall He not do it? Or hath He spoken,*
> *and shall He not make it good? (Numbers*
> *23:19).*

Therefore, there is a time coming when "the LORD thy
God will turn thy captivity, ... and gather thee from all the
nations, whither the LORD thy God hath scattered thee: ...
And the LORD thy God will bring thee into the land which
thy fathers possessed, and thou shalt possess it"
(Deuteronomy 30:3,5).

These everlasting promises to Abraham, Isaac, Jacob and
Moses were later reconfirmed to David and Solomon. God,
speaking to David concerning his son Solomon, said:

He shall build an house for my name, and I will stablish the throne of his kingdom forever ... my mercy will not depart from him, as I took it from Saul (II Samuel 7:13,15).

The ultimate fulfillment of this promise centers, of course, on the Messiah, "which was made of the seed of David according to the flesh: And declared to be the Son of God with power, ... by the resurrection from the dead" (Romans 1:3,4).

There are numerous references to these promises in the Psalms, but they become more frequent and more explicit in the books of the Prophets. Isaiah makes it clear that most of these prophecies relate not to their future return from the 70-year exile in Babylon, but to a second return—not just from Babylon but from all nations, after a much longer exile.

And it shall come to pass in that day, that the LORD shall set His hand again the second time to recover the remnant of His people ... from the four corners of the earth (Isaiah 11:11,12).

And I will bring them out from the people, and gather them from the countries, and will bring them to their own land, and feed them upon the mountains of Israel (Ezekiel 34:13).

For the children of Israel shall abide many days without a king, and without a prince, and without a sacrifice, ... Afterward shall the children of Israel return, and seek the LORD their God, and

> *David their king; and shall fear the LORD their*
> *God and His goodness in the latter days (Hosea*
> *3:4,5).*

The same theme is picked up again in the New Testament, at a time when the land of Israel was once again filled with Jews, as well as Samaritans (part Jews), and had a measure of autonomy, though actually under rather firm Roman rule. Jesus said:

> *And they shall ... be led away captive into all*
> *nations: and Jerusalem shall be trodden down*
> *of the Gentiles, until the times of the Gentiles be*
> *fulfilled: (Luke 21:24).*

Jerusalem had been under Gentile rule ever since the days of Nebuchadnezzar until it was taken by Israel from Jordan in the remarkable "Six-Day War" of 1967, and retained in the Yom Kippur War of 1973. The time of Israel's full restoration is evidently near at hand. The Apostles Peter and James, quoting the prophet Amos, said: "After this I will return, and will build again the tabernacle of David, which is fallen down: and I will build again the ruins thereof, and I will set it up" (Acts 15:16). Then, Paul said: "And so all Israel shall be saved: as it is written: There shall come out of Sion the Deliverer, and shall turn away ungodliness from Jacob" (Romans 11:26).

There are many such promises in the Bible, both explicit and implicit. The whole tenor of Scripture looks toward the ultimate restoration of Israel as God's chosen nation, once the nation repents and turns to Christ. "God hath not cast away His people which He foreknew" (Romans 11:2). Jesus said:

> *Behold your house is left unto you desolate. For I say unto you, Ye shall not see me henceforth, till ye shall say, Blessed is He that cometh in the name of the Lord (Matthew 23:38,39).*

One day soon, they (that is, the remnant of the nation that is left after the coming "time of Jacob's trouble," as prophesied in Jeremiah 30:7) will indeed acknowledge the returning Christ as their Messiah and Savior and King:

> *And I will pour upon the house of David, and upon the inhabitants of Jerusalem, the Spirit of grace and of supplications: and they shall look upon me whom they have pierced, and they shall mourn for Him, as one mourneth for his only son, ... In that day, there shall be a fountain opened to the house of David and to the inhabitants of Jerusalem for sin and for uncleanness .... And the LORD shall be king over all the earth: in that day shall there be one LORD, and His name one (Zechariah 12:10;13:1; 14:9).*

The Sign of the Fig Tree

Just three days before His crucifixion, the Lord Jesus performed a striking parabolic miracle.

> *Now in the morning as He returned into the city, He hungered. And when He saw "a fig tree in*

> *the way, He came to it, and found nothing there-*
> *on, but leaves only, and said unto it, Let no fruit*
> *grow on thee henceforward forever. And present-*
> *ly the fig tree withered away. And when the*
> *disciples saw it, they marveled, saying, How*
> *soon is the fig tree withered away! (Matthew*
> *21:18-20).*

We can be confident that Jesus was neither petty nor capricious. He certainly could have provided food for Himself and the disciples (a multitude had been fed by Him earlier). There must, therefore, be an important spiritual lesson in the withered fig tree.

This fig tree had an impressive foliage of leaves, and looked as though it should have fruit, but there was none. It was like the aprons of fig leaves fashioned by Adam and Eve in the garden (Genesis 3:7), deceptively useful as clothing, but only very temporarily able to cover their nakedness before they also would wither away.

That reference to figs was the first in the Bible. The last, in Revelation 6:19, compares a great shower of falling stars in the end-times to the phenomena when "a fig tree casteth her untimely figs, when she is shaken of a mighty wind" (Revelation 6:13). A fig tree with nothing but leaves is useless even for clothing, and a fig tree producing un-seasonable figs is like the seed on stony ground (Matthew 13:5-6, 20-21) which could bring no fruit to perfection, being unable to withstand environmental pressures and dif-ficulties.

Such was the barren fig tree encountered by Christ and His disciples that day on the Mount of Olives, and it symbolized perfectly the nation of Israel of that day, outwardly impressive but shallow and superficial, incapable of providing spiritual sustenance or protection or stability to her people, finally even rejecting her Messiah when He appeared. No wonder he cursed the fig tree! Earlier He had told them a fig tree parable, clearly indicating that this was exactly its meaning. He said:

> *A certain man had a fig tree planted in his vineyard; and he came and sought fruit therein, and found none. Then said he unto the dresser of his vineyard, Behold these three years I come seeking fruit on this fig tree, and find none; cut it down; why cumbereth it the ground? (Luke 13:6,7).*

> *For the vineyard of the LORD of hosts is the house of Israel, and the men of Judah His pleasant plant: and He looked for judgment, but behold oppression; for righteousness, but behold a cry (Isaiah 5:7).*

Not too long afterwards, Israel's "fig tree" was, indeed, cut down. The temple was destroyed by Titus in 70 A.D. and the city of Jerusalem in 135 A.D. by Hadrian, who left the whole land devastated and its people scattered to the ends of the earth.

Then began the eighteen-century long oppression of the Jewish people in almost every country on earth. Even the professing Christian church, after it became institutionalized following its own periods of intense persecution, became guilty of persecuting the Jewish people in similar fashion, calling them "Christ-killers" and slaughtering them in great numbers. Both the Roman Catholic and Eastern Orthodox churches were guilty of these atrocities, the horrors of the Spanish Inquisition and the Russian pogroms being obvious examples, though far from the only ones.

Then, of course, came the rise of the Moslem scourge, beginning with Mohammed and the Arabs just before 600 A.D., and soon sweeping across East Africa and West Asia, then all across North Africa into Spain, east into India and Indonesia, north into Turkey, southern Europe and central Asia, threatening to conquer the entire known world before it was finally halted. In the process, both Jews and Christians were either forcibly converted to Islam or slain, in very large numbers. The Jews—God's chosen people—were thus persecuted and killed almost everywhere by both Muslims and pseudo-Christians. Yet, amazingly they survived—even multiplied—and often prospered. Sad to relate, even the churches of the Reformation in many cases continued to persecute the Jews just as the Catholics had done.

Even with the beginning of significant waves of emigration to Israel after the first World War, tremendous persecution of the Jews has continued, especially in Nazi Germany, but also to some degree in Communist countries and others. Even in the nominally Christian nations of western Europe and America, considerable anti-Semitism has existed for decades. Much of this was based on the teaching that, because of Israel's rejection of Christ, she has been permanently rejected by God, with all His national promises to Israel having been "spiritualized" and transferred to the church. This has long been the predominant teaching among Catholics and the older Protestant bodies. Other Christian sects have "anglicized" the promises to Israel, maintaining that England and America constitute the so-called "lost tribes" of Israel.

An even more vitriolic anti-Semitism emanates from those groups that believe there is an underground "Zionist conspiracy" to conquer the world, supposedly documented in the almost certainly fabricated "Protocols of the Elders of Zion" and now working through the Communist international network (ignoring the fact that the great majority of Communists are Gentiles and that Communist nations such as Russia have been among the chief persecutors of Jews). Many such anti-Semitic groups base their hatred on the fiction that modern Jews are not real Jews, but are descendants of the Khazars, a tribe of uncertain ethnology that exercised considerable influence in the Caucasus area from about 200 A.D. to about 1000 A.D. Their ruling dynasty became nominal converts to Judaism in the middle of this period, but the constant warfare of the nations and religions around them eventually resulted in their extermination and/or amalgamation. Even if some of the Khazar converts to Judaism survived, they would certainly constitute, at best, a small minority among modern Jewry.

In any case, the "wandering Jew" has been persecuted almost all over the world, for more than 1800 years. "His blood be on us, and on our children" was the cry of the Jewish leaders as they pressured Pilate to crucify Jesus (Matthew 27:25), and they have surely seen the fulfillment of this imprecation! The fig tree has been barren a long, long time.

The Fig Tree Budding

But now, after almost two millennia of barrenness, the Jewish fig tree is budding again! There is no fruit yet, but the tree is budding, and this is one of the signs given by Jesus in His Olivet Discourse, when the disciples asked Him for the sign of His coming. As noted in Chapter I, He had given them the multi-sided sign of a great World War, with associated famines and pestilences and earthquakes. Then He gave them yet another sign.

Now learn a "parable" of the fig tree: When his branch is yet tender, and putteth forth leaves, ye know that summer is nigh: So likewise ye, when ye shall see all these things, know that it is near, even at the doors (Matthew 24:32–33).

The disciples could not help but tie this "parable" in with the parabolic miracle they had seen just the day before, when the barren fig tree withered away. In His parable of the fig tree recorded in Luke 13, the barren fig tree had been cut down. Yet now He was saying the fig tree would begin to bloom again. They could only take this to imply that the nation of Israel, after long being desolate and seemingly doomed to death, would eventually be revived.

This is also the teaching of the famous "dry bones" chapter in Ezekiel, when the prophet was given a vision of a valley of bones, which, at God's Word, all came together, with flesh and sinews and skins replaced on the bones, "but there was no breath in them" (Ezekiel 37:8).

God explained this strange scene thusly: "These bones are the whole house of Israel: ... Behold, O my people, I will open your graves, and cause you to come up out of your graves, and bring you into the land of Israel." (Ezekiel 37:11, 12).

These and other Scriptures tell us that, in the latter days, the people of Israel will come back to their own land. When they first return, however, they will still be in unbelief. The bones have flesh and skin, but there is no breath. The fig tree will bud, but with no fruit as yet. Eventually, however, God has said: "(I) shall put my Spirit in you, and ye shall live" (Ezekiel 37:14); the fig tree also shall bear delicious fruit. "After those days, saith the LORD. I will put my law in their inward parts, and write it in their hearts; and will be their God, and they shall be my people" (Jeremiah 31:33).

Now, of course, we only see the fig tree budding and the flesh and bones brought back together, yet without spiritual life. When we see this, however, Jesus said we could know that His coming is "near, even at the doors!" Luke's account renders His statement in slightly greater fullness. "Behold the fig tree, and all the trees; When they now shoot forth, ye see and know of your own selves that summer is nigh at hand" (Luke 21:29,30).

One could justifiably surmise that, if the fig tree suggests a revival of ancient Israel, then the phrase "all the trees" should represent Israel's other ancient neighbors in the Bible lands—such as Egypt, Babylonia (now Iraq), Persia (now Iran), Syria, Edom (now Jordan), Arabia, and others. These "trees" are budding again, too, as is Israel.

In any case, the Israeli fig tree began really to bud right after World War I, which, as we have seen, evidently constituted the first great sign of the imminent return of Christ. There were earlier waves of Jewish emigrants into Palestine (the name given the land of Israel by the Romans when they deported the Jews, naming it after the Philistines, the earlier inhabitants of the sea coast), but it began in earnest after the Balfour Declaration of 1917, naming Israel as the desired eventual homeland for the Jews.

The Turkish Ottoman Empire had controlled Israel and Jerusalem for almost 400 years when World War I broke out and Turkey entered the war on the side of Germany. The Zionist movement, under Theodore Herzl, had been urging the establishment of a Jewish homeland in Israel for two decades or more and, as a result of services rendered the British war effort by a Jewish chemist, Dr. Chaim Weizman, a semi-promise was made to do this, as implied in the Balfour Declaration.

Great Britain was given a Mandate in 1920 to govern Palestine, including much of what is now Jordan. The War had ended in 1918. Soon after the Balfour Declaration, the Turks surrendered Jerusalem to General Allenby (understood by them to mean "Allah-bey," or "Prophet of God"), without firing a shot.

The population of Jews in Israel increased steadily, the Jews purchasing tract after tract, from the Arab inhabitants. Under the industry and ingenuity of these new immigrants, the whole aspect of the land began to change. Vast groves of orange trees, modern cities, great universities and many high-tech industries, soon arose from the desolate lands.

Unfortunately, under pressure from the Arabs, England reneged on its commitment to Israel and issued a White Paper promising that the land would become an Arabic Palestinian state. The Lord apparently intervened, however, and England finally turned Palestine over to the newly formed United Nations Organization, which agreed to make Israel an independent state, partitioning Palestine into two nations, one Jewish and one Arabic. England pulled out, and Israel declared her independent statehood in May 1948.

The Arabs, however, had totally rejected the possibility of an Israeli state in their midst, and immediately began fighting to drive all the Jews into the sea, a resolve most of them maintain to this day. Egypt, Jordan, Iraq, Syria and Lebanon, all immediately went to war with Israel.

Despite apparently overwhelming Arab superiority in both weapons and numbers, however, Israel eventually won the war, which ended in February 1949, Israel having won much more territory than had been originally allotted her in the U.N. partition.

The Arabic nations did not give up, however, nor have they to this day. In 1956, Egypt attacked again, but Israel quickly won the Sinai War. Then, in June 1967, the remarkable Six-Day War took place, with Israel rapidly defeating the armies of Egypt, Syria, Jordan and Iraq. In this war, Israel took the West Bank area of Jordan, Sinai and the Gaza Strip from Egypt and the Golan Heights from Syria, as well as great amounts of Russian-made weaponry. Especially important was Israel's conquest of the Old City of Jerusalem from Jordan.

Then came the Yom Kippur War in October 1973, in which Israel—again immensely outnumbered in weapons and manpower—was attacked by Egypt and Syria. Israel prevailed, however, in a war lasting 19 days this time. Then, when Iraq attacked Kuwait in 1990, every attempt was made by Iraq to get Israel into the fray, attacking her with a long series of deadly SCUD missiles. Israel refrained from entering this war, and the U.N. coalition eventually completely defeated the Iraqis.

These have been only the major conflicts, with minor fighting, terrorism and tensions a continual problem in Israel. Nevertheless, the little nation has become very strong and productive, beautiful and fruitful. The fig tree, indeed, is budding abundantly, and summer must be near!

But it is still largely an atheistic nation, although there is now a growing minority of Orthodox Jews there, and even a small contingent of Christian Jews. American Christian tourists have come in droves, and Bibles and Christian literature are available to the Israelis in large numbers. Much seed has been sown, and someday there will be a great harvest of spiritual fruit on the revived and budding tree.

The Time of Jacob's Trouble

Before the fig tree yields its fruit, however, and before the dry bones truly receive the Spirit of life, the children of Israel must endure one more time of great persecution, worse than any before it. Note what the prophets have said:

> *Alas! for that day is great, so that none is like it: it is even the time of Jacob's trouble, but he shall be saved out of it (Jeremiah 30:7).*

> *And at that time ... there shall be a time of trouble, such as never was since there was a nation even to that same time; and at that time thy people shall be delivered, every one that shall be found written in the book (Daniel 12:1).*

> *When ye therefore shall see the abomination of desolation, spoken of by Daniel the prophet, stand in the holy place, ... Then let them which be in Judea flee unto the mountains: ... For then shall be great tribulation, such as was not since the beginning of the world to this time, no, nor ever shall be (Matthew 24:15,16,21).*

This greatest of all periods of tribulation for the Jews is clearly yet in the future. Also, it is obvious in the context of each of these prophecies that their setting is in the land of Israel. We have already shown (Chapter 2), from the prophecy in Ezekiel 38, that Gog's invasion of Israel in the last days occurs only after the Jewish people have returned to the land while still in unbelief—not even believing in a personal God. Their miraculous deliverance, however, will persuade the whole nation to abandon their atheism and pantheism and return to belief in the God of their fathers.

Sadly, however, they will still reject Jesus as their Messiah, and thus God must bring against them this final "time of Jacob's trouble"; then, finally, "He shall be saved out of it"—in fact, as Paul said, "all Israel shall be saved" (Romans 11:26).

This is the condition of the land today. The Israelis have reestablished their nation in the land, but the great majority—especially their leaders—do not even believe in a personal God, especially not in Jesus Christ as their Creator/Savior, and so are still lost in unbelief, awaiting with great concern the threat of an imminent invasion by Russia and her Moslem allies.

It is remarkable that the Jews have controlled the city of Jerusalem for almost 25 years now, ever since the 1967 Six-Day War. Thus it would seem that Christ's prophecy had been fulfilled, when He predicted that "Jerusalem would be trodden down of the Gentiles, until the times of the Gentiles be fulfilled" (Luke 21:24). With Jerusalem back in Jewish hands for the first time since the days of Nebuchadnezzar, it seems that they should also have accepted Christ and the Messianic kingdom finally established.

The problem is that the most important part of Jerusalem—the one area that really makes it the Holy City—is still trodden down of the Gentiles. This is the site of the Temple, the place where God "dwelt" and met with His people, the tract purchased by David from Araunah for this purpose, the mount where Father Abraham long ago had offered up Isaac. That one indispensable site *is* Jerusalem, in God's sight, but it is still desecrated by the "Dome of the Rock" and the "Mosque of Omar," firmly under Moslem control, not even accessible to the Jews at all. It would seem that Israel could easily take the Temple Mount from the Arabs and rebuild their temple, as an Orthodox minority is currently urging her to do. But, knowing that such an action would immediately bring down the extreme wrath of the whole Moslem world—supported by Russia—on her head, and since the leaders and intellectuals of the land don't really want the temple restored anyhow, the Moslems remain in control of the real Jerusalem.

In fact, it will evidently take this terrible time of Jacob's trouble, preceded by the invasion and defeat of the Russian/Moslem confederacy, to change this situation. Jerusalem must still undergo a time of great tribulation before it can finally become the true "City of Peace" and the fig tree can bear good fruit.

The Creation of Israel

This will be accomplished, however, by the end of the great tribulation period, when a nation will be born in a day, as it were, and all the people will "mourn" for the One "whom they have pierced" (Zechariah 12:10), perhaps making the great Confession of Isaiah 53:3–12, especially verse 6: "All we like sheep have gone astray: we have turned every one to his own way; and the LORD hath laid on Him the iniquity of us all."

During this period of unprecedented persecution, the Lord will call out 144,000 "servants of our God," 12,000 from each of the twelve tribes of Israel (Revelation 7:4–8), and these presumably will bear witness to their brethren during the tribulation, preparing them to receive Christ when He finally appears at its end. Perhaps even now the Lord is using the testimony of the few Christians in Israel, and especially the Bibles and Christian literature which have been planted as good seed in the land, to prepare these 144,000 future witnesses.

The amazing imminent conversion of the whole nation to Christ, coming on top of the long miraculous history of the land and its people, as we have outlined it in this chapter, makes it so unique that God actually calls it a special creation.

> *But be ye glad and rejoice forever in that which I create: for, behold, I create Jerusalem a rejoicing, and her people a joy (Isaiah 65:18).*

The terminology of creation (the Hebrew word *bara*, meaning "create," always has "God" as its subject, for creation is a work only God can do) is normally reserved only for the primeval creation or some other mighty supernatural creative act of God (e.g., the "new creation" of a soul born again through faith in Christ). In this special case of redeemed Israel and Jerusalem, however, so many supernatural acts of God have been required through the ages to form and preserve the nation of Israel that the term "creation" becomes beautifully and singularly appropriate.

When the LORD shall build up Zion, He shall appear in His glory.... This shall be written for the generation to come: and the people which shall be created shall praise the LORD (Psalm 102:16,18).

CHAPTER 4

Back to Babel

The Rebuilding of Babylon

Another remarkable sign of the approaching end is the rebuilding of the ancient city of Babylon. Next to Jerusalem, Babylon is the most frequently mentioned city in the Bible, and was the inveterate enemy of God's people in Israel. It is noteworthy that both cities were to be rebuilt and come into great prominence again in the last days.

In addition to their physical significance, each has a profound spiritual and symbolic role. Paul wrote about the "Jerusalem which is above ... the mother of us all" (Galatians 4:26), and John called Babylon "the mother of harlots and abominations of the earth" (Revelation 17:5). The eternal Holy City, where all the redeemed will dwell forever, is called "new Jerusalem" (Revelation 21:2), whereas Babylon is "a destroying mountain" and "the hammer of the whole earth" (Jeremiah 51:25; 50:23).

Because of her wickedness, cruelty and idolatry, Isaiah predicted her doom and destruction over a century before she reached the zenith of her power, and then invaded Israel.

Babylon, the glory of kingdoms ... shall be as when God overthrew Sodom and Gomorrah. It shall never be inhabited, neither shall it be dwelt in from generation to generation: neither shall the Arabian pitch tent there; ... (Isaiah 13:19,20).

Then, a hundred years later, after many Jews had already been carried into exile in Babylon, and Nebuchadnezzar had burned down Jerusalem and its holy temple, Jeremiah prophesied in similar vein.

How is the hammer of the whole earth cut asunder and broken! how is Babylon become a desolation among the nations! ... and it shall be no more inhabited for ever; ... (Jeremiah 50:23, 39).

Many other such prophecies told of the coming fall of Babylon and her perpetual desolation,but they have never yet been completely fulfilled. Babylon was never destroyed suddenly "as when God overthrew Sodom and Gomorrah," and even today the Iraqi Arabs are "pitching their tents there," as it were, in the process of rebuilding the city, and it is "being inhabited" again in our own generation. It did, indeed, gradually fall into almost complete decay about a century after Christ, but has never been completely uninhabited, with small Arab settlements scattered here and there among the ruins of its former glory, ever since its heyday.

In the last great prophetic book of the Bible, as the Apostle John was translated forward in time to the last days, he saw Babylon as "that great city, which reigneth over the kings of the earth" and as "that great city, that was clothed in fine linen, and purple, and scarlet, and decked with gold, and precious stones, and pearls" (Revelation 17:18;18:16). He then saw the kings of the earth, over whom she was ruling, turn and "burn her with fire," so that "her plagues (shall) come in one day, death, and mourning, and famine; and she shall be utterly burned with fire" (Revelation 17:16; 18:8). In essence, John was repeating the ancient prophecies of Isaiah and Jeremiah. The latter had been fulfilled precursively and partially, in accord with the common Biblical principle of prophetic double reference, but their final, complete fulfillment is still future. At that time "Babylon shall become heaps, a dwelling place for dragons, an astonishment, and an hissing, without an inhabitant." " ... the habitation of devils, and the hold of every foul spirit, and a cage of every unclean and hateful bird" (Jeremiah 51:37; Revelation 18:2). Then, finally, "the sea is come up upon Babylon; she is covered with the multitude of the waves thereof," for "a mighty angel took up a stone like a millstone, and cast it into the sea, saying, Thus with violence shall that great city Babylon be thrown down, and shall be found no more at all" (Jeremiah 51:42; Revelation 18:21).

Thus it is profoundly significant that the "madman of Baghdad," Saddam Hussein, the recent dictatorial president of Iraq (which formerly was known as Mesopotamia, the land "between the rivers"), occupying the same geographic territory as ancient Babylonia and Assyria, has been using many of his oil billions on a gigantic project with the goal of rebuilding Babylon as it was in its glory days under Nebuchadnezzar.

The project was first conceived in the early 1950's, just after Iraq began to develop her oil resources, with the primary aim of creating a tourist attraction. It proceeded slowly, however, until Saddam came into power in 1979. He started the war with Iran in 1980, then in 1982 began an intense effort to restore Babylon. Both of these projects were, to him, historical symbols of national pride and destiny. The first was to redress the ancient conquest of Babylon by Persia, which had marked the end of the great Babylonian empire. The second was to serve, he hoped, as the capital of all the Arab nations. His dream was to unite all Arabs—and eventually all Muslims—in a mighty empire which would someday conquer the world. He envisioned himself as the successor to Emperor Nebuchadnezzar, and intensively promoted this theme among the Iraqi people—especially in the rebuilt streets and palaces of Babylon—ever since he came into power.

He failed in his eight-year war against Persia (Iran), however, and he will fail even more miserably in his dream of ruling the world from Babylon as the new Nebuchadnezzar.

He will, sooner or later, go the way of all flesh. He could be destroyed by his own people, who are increasingly desperate after their eight years of great suffering in the war with Iran, followed almost immediately by his incredibly costly and deadly war with the United States and the U.N. coalition when he invaded Kuwait. If he survives this disaster, only to consort with "Gog" in the coming Russo/Moslem invasion of Israel (see Ezekiel 38–39, and Chapter 2 of this book), his armies will be wiped out on the mountains of Israel. Either way, Saddam will soon come to his end.

But Babylon will still be there, on the Euphrates River, 55 miles south of Bagdad. At this writing, her restoration is only partially—though substantially—complete, and apparently was not damaged during Iraq's two wars. Saddam Hussein will not fulfill his dream of empire there, but another will!

The United States of Europe

Assuming that Russia and the Moslem states will be so decisively beaten in Israel that they cannot again become a serious threat to the world, a great power vacuum will be left in the Middle East as well as eastern and northern Europe. The oil riches of the Arab states, which are absolutely vital to the industrial economies of both Europe and the Far East (especially Japan, China and Korea) will be an irresistible magnet.

The nations of western Europe will probably be the ones who move in to claim the prize, having the advantage by this time of a strong union. Soon after World War II, the North Atlantic Treaty Organization (NATO) was formed as a military alliance. This, however, included the United States as an important, perhaps the dominant, member.

The European Common Market, on the other hand, first formed in 1957, is strictly a tight economic union of ten or more nations of western Europe, from Greece to the United Kingdom, and including such major powers as France, Germany and Italy. This European Community, as it is officially called, now has its own Parliament and its common European Currency Unit (ECU). In many areas of activity, there has been strong pressure towards the formation of a full-scale political union, almost comparable to what might be called the United States of Europe. They will, together, have military, economic and numerical strength comparable to those of either the Soviet Union or the United States of America.

This remarkable development of a European Union has been interpreted by many teachers of Bible prophecy to be the initiation of their long-anticipated revival of the old Roman Empire. A better name for this development, however, might be the Revised Roman Empire, for the old Roman Empire involved far more than these ten states of western Europe. It included all the nations bordering the Mediterranean, extending through Belgium and England on the west and Armenia and Iraq on the east, but did not include Russia,

Persia or any more distant lands. Any supposed correlation of Rome's former empire with the Common Market nations is tenuous and partial, at best. The Roman empire never incorporated what are now the Common Market nations of Germany, Denmark, Ireland, or Netherlands, but did include all North Africa, Syria and Israel.

The concept of a revived Roman empire hangs almost entirely on the prophetic image in Nebuchadnezzar's dream, as interpreted by Daniel (see Daniel 2:31-45). According to this prophecy, from Daniel's time onward, there was to be a succession of four dominant world empires—Babylonia, Persia, Greece and Rome in order, plus another that seemed to be part Roman empire, part modern democracy. The latter is then to be succeeded by the Messianic kingdom of Christ at His second coming. Now, since the Old Roman empire disintegrated long ago, yet in Nebuchadnezzar's image seemed still to exist at Christ's return, it has been assumed that the Roman empire must be revived. In the early years of this century, in fact, it was widely believed by Christians that Mussolini, Italy's dictator, would be the Antichrist, since his ambition was to rebuild Rome's ancient empire. Mussolini died in degradation, however, as have Hitler and various other alleged "antichrists."

The fact is that the Roman empire, in its most significant later phases, never died, so does not need to be revived. Although it does not have a single capital city or human ruler, its legal system has become the model for most modern law codes, its military and governmental systems are widely copied, Graeco/Roman philosophy dominates modern education, and its religion and culture are largely perpetuated in the Roman and Greek Catholic churches. As suggested by the feet of the image, its rigid autocracy has been largely mixed with democracy and even socialism in its successor nations, but the Roman empire in its essence has persisted to the present day. In fact, it has extended into the Americas and Australia, and it even dominated north Africa and the Middle East until the Moslem invasions changed those nations into an Islamic culture. Thus the "Roman" portion of Daniel's image could be interpreted to mean not only the nations of western Europe, but any great western confederacy that will seek to fill the Middle East power vacuum after the coming fall of Russia and her Moslem client states when Gog invades Israel.

Without attempting at this point to describe this coming Western Union of nations more specifically, it is certainly possible that at least some members of the European Community (Common Market) will be heavily involved in it, but so may the United States—or even Egypt and Arabia (since these and the other Persian Gulf oil states will apparently not participate in Gog's invasion).

Another prophecy in Daniel throws possible further light on the end time situation. In Daniel 7, the prophet had a vision of the four winds striving on the great sea—evidently the Mediterranean. Then "four great beasts" came up from the sea (verse 3), presumably striving like the four winds that brought them up.

This prophecy is often interpreted in parallel with the image-dream of Nebuchadnezzar, with the four beasts representing the same four kingdoms as the image. This interpretation would make this a somewhat redundant prophecy, however, and it seems more likely that the beasts are four great rival confederacies in the latter days. They seem to emerge from the sea simultaneously and in fact, the fourth beast is slain before the three which preceded it (verse 11,12). All four, at the time of Daniel's writing, were still future (verse 17), whereas Babylon had already fallen and Persia had already succeeded it by that time.

"The first was like a lion, and had eagle's wings" (verse 4). Nations quite commonly symbolize themselves by animals, and this beast might represent an alliance of the British lion and the American eagle in the last days. "A second, like to a bear, ... had three ribs in the mouth of it," attempting to "devour much flesh." (verse 5). One naturally thinks here of the Russian bear, before its coming disaster in Israel. Then, "lo another, like a leopard," with four wings and four heads (verse 6). This strange beast may represent a confederation of the pantheistic nations of the Far East (e.g., Japan, China), for these also would have great need of the oil riches of the Persian Gulf region. There are certain other references to the potential threat from the Far East (Daniel 11:44; Revelation 16:12).

The fourth is a nondescript beast, "dreadful and terrible" (verse 7), possibly the same beast later described arising out of the sea by John. "The beast which I saw was like unto a leopard, and his feet were as the feet of a bear, and his mouth as the mouth of a lion" (Revelation 13:2).

The "beast" seen by John was soon to become the world ruler for 3½ years, and is seen by him as a composite of the first three "beasts" described by Daniel, indicating evidently that the fourth "beast" will prevail over all the great confederations that will have warred against him.

In any case, whatever the final configuration of nations may be, the scriptures imply that their beast ruler will appropriate Babylon for his capital. He will probably reject the use of any current capital city, for he will aspire to world dominion, and Babylon would be ideal for this purpose. Since Babylon is very close to the geographic center of all the earth's land masses, it would provide the optimum location for a world center of finance, transportation and communication, as well as political controls. As the first great capital of all mankind, it would be appropriate to designate it as the capital of the United Nations and a one-world government. "The fourth beast ... shall devour the whole earth, ... and they shall be given into his hand until a time and times and the dividing of time" [that is, 3½ years] (Daniel 7:23,25). "And power was given unto (the beast) to continue forty and two months" (Revelation 13:5).

Whatever remains to be completed in the rebuilding of Babylon can be quickly accomplished with the oil billions the Beast will have acquired in his conquests, using the most modern construction technology, as well as all the slave labor he may demand. Babylon will quickly become a major metropolis, with people from every nation in her streets and shops and entertainment centers. Both the glories of ancient Babylon and the luxuries of modern technology will be evident everywhere, and so also will flourish the whole gamut of both ancient and modern ungodliness and immorality—but only for a brief time!

World Religion and the New Age Movement

The Beast, as he is called in both Daniel and Revelation, is also called "that man of sin ... the son of perdition" by Paul (II Thessalonians 2:3). He is a man, very likely alive today and soon to be revealed in his true character, but he is also a Satan-possessed man (Revelation 13:4), energized by Satan and prepared by him for the specific role of ruling the world for Satan and destroying all faith in the true Creator God and Savior Jesus Christ. Thus, he will seek to establish a worldwide antitheistic religious system as well as a world government. Ultimately, in fact, his goal (and Satan's goal) is to establish universal acceptance of Satan as "God." His "minister of religion" is still another "beast," also called "the false prophet" (Revelation 13:11; 16:13), whose function will be to promote and enforce a religion of evolutionary pantheistic humanism, focused especially on worshiping "Man" as the highest achievement of the intelligent Cosmos in its evolutionary progress through the ages. "Man" in general is personified in this representative man who will rule the world in the name of Satan (or Lucifer) the "god of this world" (II Corinthians 4:4), who is himself the alleged soul of the eternal Cosmos.

It is not surprising, therefore, that another sign of the last days is the so called "New-Age Movement," now sweeping over the world like wildfire. This is not a homogeneous and cohesive movement, by any means, but involves a wide spectrum of cults and beliefs and organizations—some in science, some in business, some in education, some in medicine, many in occult religion and philosophy, something for everyone! But two beliefs are common to all New-Age concepts—belief in evolution and belief in world government.

The scientific revolution was born in the context of Christian theism, primarily through the work of great creationist scientists such as Isaac Newton, Robert Boyle, James Joule, Blaise Pascal and many others of like mind. It was not long, however, before men such as Charles Lyell, Charles Darwin and other materialistic scientists and philosophers led the world into the morass of gross naturalism and deism, thence into atheism.

Eventually, however, it became so obvious that random processes could never produce a complex universe, and that evolution by gradual changes preserved through natural selection was so devoid of scientific evidence, that people (particularly young people) began to rebel in large numbers against traditional Darwinian evolutionary humanism.

Unfortunately, although many are returning today to belief in true creationism and Biblical Christianity, even more are turning to one or another New Age faith. All of the New Age cults and practices repudiate Biblical Christianity, of course (though some try to mask this as they seek to infiltrate evangelical churches and para-church organizations), but they also repudiate traditional atheism and evolution-by-chance. Instead, they advocate some form of pantheism, attributing intelligence to Mother Nature or the Cosmos, directing evolution through a pantheon of spirit-beings that had evolved in former ages. In reality, New Age beliefs are not new at all, but merely a revival of ancient paganism expressed in modern jargon. Since the Cosmos itself is "god," every component thereof is a part of deity, and the emphasis in the New Age is that every human being should come to this divine consciousness of his or her own divinity. This, of course, is evolutionary humanism in full flower. In worshiping some guru or religious leader or dictator, people are actually worshiping themselves. This movement will eventually culminate in the worship of such a "Man" as king of the earth, who (they believe) will bring about global harmony.

One prominent current candidate being touted by many "New-Agers" for this role is a man called Lord Maitreya, reputed to be a reincarnation of Buddha and of Christ. He is said now to be the leader of a mystic Islamic cult in a Pakistani community in London, destined shortly to be revealed to the world as Christ in His second coming. He is, no doubt, merely one of the "false Christs" warned of by the true Lord Jesus Christ in His Olivet Discourse, but many today believe in Him, and he is claimed to have talked at length with President George Bush and President

Gorbachev. He has been for some time a popular symbol among the New Age Mystics.

ᵛ In any case, it would be natural for this abundance of New-Age cults and movements to come eventually together in a great "Back-to-Babel" movement. Babel was the center of the world's first anti-God religion and first world government, so it would be profoundly significant to them to establish what they hope will be the final and permanent system of world culture there.

As a foretoken of this, a great gathering of such people was held in rebuilt Babylon on September 22, 1987, a date selected by Saddam Hussein because it was the seventh anniversary of his invasion of Iran. This was primarily planned as a cultural festival, featuring dancers and musicians from all over the world. Another was held a year later. There were great processions and dramatic performances. The opening ceremonies included a play eulogizing the Babylonian mother goddess Ishtar, and the final procession marched through the reconstructed Ishtar Gate for another great tribute to the goddess. Amazingly, there was no significant opposition to this by the supposedly monotheistic Muslims.

This annual festival has been halted for the present, however, as Saddam Hussein had to divert his attention to the immediate problem of refilling his treasuries, depleted after the eight-year war with Iran. He proceeded to pressure the rulers of the small but wealthy country of Kuwait to raise their oil prices, then invaded their country when they refused, with disastrous consequences that now have essentially terminated his grandiose plans for a new Babylonian empire.

The rebuilding of Babylon is, therefore, currently on hold, but this is only temporary. It will soon be under way again, though probably as an international project rather than merely to satisfy Saddam's narcissistic dreams of empire. All that has been happening in the restored Babylon so far, however, is surely an emblematic foreshadowing of what is to come.

In the meantime, the New Age movement, which few people were even aware of fifteen years ago, is rapidly becoming a dominant force in human society everywhere. It embraces an extremely wide spectrum of cults and activities—from witchcraft, astrology, spiritism and Satanism at one end of the spectrum, all the way to scientific concepts such as the Gaia hypothesis of the geologists, the biogenetic and morphogenetic fields of the biologists, and the anthropic principle of the cosmologists on the other. All are founded upon the concept of evolution, all are globalist in philosophy and goals, all are pantheistic in spirit and humanistic in worship. All reject the concept of a transcendent personal Creator God, all reject the Bible as the inerrant Word of God, all reject the incarnation of God in man in the person of the Lord Jesus Christ, all reject the substitutionary death of Christ on the cross for human sin, all reject His bodily resurrection from the dead, all reject the gift of salvation and eternal life through faith in the person and work of Jesus Christ, and all—despite their professed commitment to the idea of universal love and brotherhood—hate with great intensity "fundamentalists" who believe and teach the above truths.

The doctrines and practices of the New Age vary widely, and they often quarrel with each other and with the atheists and secular humanists, but they are all united with them in their fundamental rejection of the true God and the true Christ. They will all eventually merge with each other and with their spiritual forebears, the ethnic religions of the East (Hinduism, Buddhism, Taoism, etc.) in the great world religious system of the ultimate Antichrist—the Beast of the book of Revelation, and the Man of Sin.

The list of New Age cults (really age-old pantheistic religions of Satan revitalized) thriving in today's world is almost endless. They include secret societies such as the Free Masons, religious denominations such as Christian Science, Unity, Mormonism, Religious Science, Unitarianism, etc., pseudo-scientific religions such as Scientology, Transcendental Meditation, Spiritism, etc., and innumerable other groups. (See the book *New Age Cults and Religions*, by Texe Marrs for a description of over 100 of them.) Their adherents number in the millions, and they influence many other millions, in literally every nation of the world. Their proposed global religion could become a reality very soon.

Mother of Abominations

Saddam Hussein proclaimed foolishly that his armies would produce "the mother of all battles" in his fight to establish his new Babylon as capital of a pan-Arabic empire. Perhaps he was inadvertently led to such a phrase from the Biblical reference to Babylon as "the mother of harlots and abominations of the earth" (Revelation 17:5).

Actually, this colorful phrase was applied to "Mystery Babylon the Great," indicating that something more than the literal city of Babylon—whether the ancient city or the rebuilt city—was in view. The word for "abomination" in the Bible, in both Old and New Testaments, applies especially to idol-worship and the immoral practices associated with it. The word for "harlots" can apply to any form of sexual behavior outside of the divinely established institution of marriage. Various kinds of illicit sexual behavior have almost always accompanied idolatry, and these apparently all did originate (in the post-flood world, at least), in the city of Babel, established and ruled by Nimrod, Noah's great-grandson through Cush and Ham (Genesis 10:8–10).

The primary thrust of this ascription is undoubtedly to Babel as the originator of idolatry, which is nothing more nor less than spiritual adultery, serving Satan and loving his ways more than the true Creator God. It has been well documented (see *The Two Babylons* by Alexander Hislop, as well as my own book, *The Long War against God*) that Babel, or Babylon, was indeed the corrupt source from which all the false religions in the post-flood world, as well as all evil practices, were originally derived.

The gods and goddesses worshiped in the various ancient nations of the world (Egypt, India, Greece, Rome, etc.) were practically the same (though with different names) as those in ancient Babylon. This important fact has been noted by many authorities on mythology and world religions. It is not so widely known, however, that all these are actually personifications of natural systems, activities, and forces—the god of the sea, the goddess of fertility, the god of war, etc. By the actions and relations of these cosmic beings—that is, the forces and systems of "Mother Nature"—the world, with all its animals and people, was supposedly brought into its present form from a primeval watery chaos. This concept is found in most ancient cosmogonic myths, but the whole concept is nothing but evolutionism. It is pantheistic evolutionism, of course, not the atheistic evolutionism of the Darwinians, neo-Darwinians and punctuationists of the past century. Although it rejects the truth of supernatural creation and a personal God, it assumes that the eternal cosmos of space, time and matter (personified as Mother Nature or Mother Earth or Father Time or something) is somehow conscious and capable of generating the world and all things, including gods, spirits, people and animals. The spirits so produced were also identified as gods and goddesses, with their homes in the heavens, essentially identical with the stars and planets, which thus were capable of influencing human lives and destinies. These spirits of the gods were, on occasion, able to communicate (sometimes even to consort) with men and women, and vast legends of their exploits, as well as the practices of astrology, animism and other occult sciences, grew up around this basic concept.

This monstrous system of evolutionary pantheism, accompanied by polytheism, astrology, spiritism, animism and eventually humanism, atheism and Satanism, thus originated at Babel and was spread throughout the world when God confused the languages and dispersed the unified population there around the earth (Genesis 11:9). It has assumed varied forms in different times and places, but has always been essentially the same. In modern times, it took the form of the pseudo-science called Darwinian evolution, but the scientific impossibilities associated with this (or any other) form of atheistic evolutionism are now causing a reaction against it, and encouraging a return to the original evolutionary pantheism of King Nimrod at Babel, under the guise of the "New-Age" Movement.

Evolutionism has been the basic weapon in Satan's long war against God, from ancient Babel to modern times. In turn, it has served as the pseudo-scientific rationale, not only for the abominations associated with idolatry and the other practices of the ancient pagan religions and their modern "children" in the form of the various modern ethnic religions, but also for wars, exploitation, slavery, abortionism, sexual promiscuity, drug use, and almost every evil system or practice known to man (see *The Long War against God* for detailed documentation). No wonder the angel speaking to John called this system with all its deadly products Mystery Babylon the Great, Mother of Harlots and Abominations of the Earth. Transmitted originally through the rebel Nimrod (who was probably later deified by the Sumerians and Babylonians as the god Merodach, or

Marduk), this system must originally have been revealed to him by the evil "host of heaven," the fallen angels, led by Lucifer himself—that old Serpent, Satan, or the Devil—who aspires to "ascend into heaven" and to be "like the most High" (Isaiah 14:13). Even though God cast him out of heaven with all the rebel angels who followed him, he still is seeking to defeat God through corrupting the world of human beings whom God had created in His own image (Genesis 1:27).

It seems probable that Satan's rationale for believing he can dethrone his Creator is by refusing to believe that God *is* his Creator. He chose instead to believe that both he and God had evolved out of the primeval watery "chaos" which had been the environment of his first awareness when God created him (compare Genesis 1:2; Psalm 104:1-4; Ezekiel 28:13-15; etc). Thus Satan himself was the first evolutionary pantheist, and he has used this same self-deception ever since to seduce men and women as well as his own coterie of demonic spirits, beginning again at Babel after God had cleansed the first world with the great flood.

This spirit of Babel has blanketed the world through all subsequent ages, and so has been called "Mystery Babylon." But the primeval city itself, the chief national enemy of God's people from Nimrod to Nebuchadnezzar, will also be revived in the last days, under "another Nimrod," a Satan-possessed and controlled "Man of Sin." This "son of perdition" will make Babylon once again the world's center of government, of finance, of culture, industry, trade, communications, education and false religion, accompanied by all the harlotry and abominations of the ages. Mystery Babylon will again be centered in, and one with, commercial Babylon.

The Rise and Fall of Babylon

The Iraqi dictator, Saddam Hussein, with his dreams of empire, began to rebuild Babylon, but he could not finish it. One day soon, however, the great capitals of government, finance, culture and religion (in New York, London, Rome, Geneva, etc.) will all move their ungodly systems back to their ancestral home in Babylon. The prophet Zechariah saw this in a vision 2400 years ago.

And, there was lifted up a talent of lead; and this is a woman that sitteth in the midst of the ephah. And he said, This is wickedness. And he cast it into the midst of the ephah; and he cast the weight of lead upon the mouth thereof. Then lifted I up mine eyes, and looked, and, behold, there came out two women, and the wind was in their wings; for they had wings like the wings of a stork: and they lifted up the ephah between the earth and the heaven. Then said I to the angel that talked with me. Whither do these bear the ephah? And he said unto me, To build it an house in the land of Shinar: and it shall be established, and set there upon her own base (Zechariah 5:7–11).

The "ephah" in this vision was a measuring basket, symbolic of commerce, but the contents of the ephah consisted only of a woman said to be symbolic of wickedness. A lead weight capping the container would assure that this woman of wickedness would be confined therein until she was returned to "her own base" in the "land of Shinar," being translated there by two stork-like women (the stork was considered an unclean bird).

Shinar, of course, is where Nimrod first built Babel and its base of wickedness (Genesis 11:2). The vision thus indicates that the world's great cup of wickedness and covetousness, centered for so long in Babylon, then Persia and Greece and Rome, and finally in the extended Roman influence throughout the western world (as shown in Nebuchadnezzar's image), was finally to be brought back to Babel where it all started. When it does happen, it will happen very quickly, as indicated by the great wings, aided as it were by a mighty wind, transporting it there.

That this vision was for the end-times is evident in the context. This was the ninth in a series of ten visions given to the prophet Zechariah. The seventh vision, one of two olive trees symbolizing "two anointed ones" (Zechariah 4:2,3,14) will not be specifically fulfilled until it is fulfilled by the two end-time witnesses just before the Beast achieves full control over the earth for 3½ years (Revelation 11:3-4; 13:4-5). Babylon, therefore, will evidently be established as such a center just at this time, when the two witnesses have been removed and the Beast finally will rule the world.

This corresponds to the awesome scene in Revelation 17 and 18. There "Mystery Babylon," Zechariah's woman of wickedness, is seen now as "the great whore" (17:1), no longer sitting in the ephah basket, but sitting on "many waters" which are then explained as "peoples, and multitudes, and nations, and tongues" (17:15). She is also called "that great city, which reigneth over the kings of the earth" (17:18). She is clothed in great wealth, but is drunk "with the blood of the martyrs of Jesus" (17:4,6). She can be nothing less than the Satanic religious system of Nimrod and Nebuchadnezzar and of all the kings and peoples subservient to this system through the ages, finally come home again to her ancient house in Babel, where she holds the world under her control in the abominable religious system of pantheistic evolutionism and idolatrous wickedness.

Then, somehow, we see the Beast, upon whom the woman was riding into power (17:3), later turning on her, persuading ten kings also to follow him (17:12–13). "These shall hate the whore, and shall make her desolate and naked, and shall eat her flesh, and burn her with fire" (17:16). From thenceforth the Beast will no longer support the great complex of New-Age religions, ethnic religions, apostate Christian religions, humanistic philosophies, Islamic religions, etc., which have served through the ages as "Mystery Babylon." The time will have come to turn the world over to full-fledged Satanism, thus fulfilling Lucifer's primal ambition to be recognized as "God." "And they worshiped the Dragon which gave power to the Beast" (Revelation 13:4).

But this absolute reign will be short-lived, for very soon we see, in Revelation 18, the total destruction of the physical city of Babylon itself, not just her religious trappings. The city and "the merchants of the earth" (18:11), who have become incredibly wealthy through their Babylonian commerce, who "were made rich by her" (18:12-15), will suddenly be destroyed "in one hour" (18:10,19).

The agent of destruction is probably not a nuclear bomb, although the destruction sounds similar to what such a bomb would accomplish. In some unspecified way, but one which will leave no doubt as to its divine source, she will die, "for strong is the Lord God who judgeth her" (18:8).

This will occur very near the end of the coming period of great tribulation. The city already will have suffered under some of the plagues of that period, but her rich trade and the profligate life style of her residents will have continued in defiance of God, who will be assumed by them to have been deposed by Satan and their king, the Beast.

Suddenly, this will all be gone, and there will be great mourning by those who watch Babylon burning from afar. It is noteworthy that one of the greatest losses, in the minds of these mourners, will be the cessation of the great musical festivals held there—ever since the first one sponsored by Saddam Hussein back in 1987. "The voice of harpers, and musicians, and of pipers, and trumpeters, shall be heard no more at all in thee," they will cry (18:22). It is remarkable what a hold ungodly music has on the hearts of ungodly people.

The destruction of the great capital will have been preceded by the destruction of other cities of the world in the greatest earthquake in earth history (Revelation 16:18–19), so the world will be in shambles by this time. But the end is not quite yet. "The kings of the earth and of the whole world" are being gathered together (Revelation 16:16) toward a great plain in the land of Israel "called in the Hebrew tongue Armageddon," and the Lord Jesus Christ will be meeting them there!

CHAPTER 5

Seven Years of Fury

The Seventieth Week

One of the most amazing prophecies in the Bible is found in Daniel 9—the famous prophecy of the seventy weeks, sent by God to the prophet Daniel via the angel Gabriel.

Seventy weeks [literally, 'seventy sevens'] are determined upon thy people and upon thy holy city ... from the going forth of the commandment to restore and to build Jerusalem unto the Messiah the Prince shall be seven weeks, and threescore and two weeks: the street shall be built again and the wall, even in troublous times. And after threescore and two weeks shall Messiah be cut off, but not for Himself: and the people of the prince that shall come shall destroy the city and the sanctuary; and the end thereof shall be with a flood, and unto the end of the war, desolations are determined (Daniel 9:24–26).

Although there have been several different interpretations of this prophecy, it is best simply to take it literally and in context. Daniel had been assuming that the seventy years of Judah's captivity were about over, but then Gabriel told him that it was not seventy years, but seventy sevens of years—that is, 490 years—during which God would be counting the time for Israel's final return from exile.

The first 69 of these weeks (or 483 years) would be the time between the command of Artaxerxes "to restore and to build Jerusalem" (a command which, according to the standard chronology, was given in 446 B.C.—note Nehemiah 2:1-8) to the coming of Messiah as "prince" (a word more commonly translated "ruler" or "leader"). The "prophetic year," the same as the year as primevaly created, before the great flood, was 360 days long. Correcting for this factor, and for the fact that Jesus was actually born in 4 B.C. and that the year following 1 B.C. was 1 A.D., the date of this promised coming of Messiah is calculated at about 30 A.D., when He was 33½ years old, the very time when He entered Jerusalem presenting Himself as Judah's promised King Messiah. A week later, however, He was "cut off" [that is, 'executed'], but "not for Himself."

This remarkable prophetic fulfillment completed the first 483 years of the 490-year prophecy. That the final seven years, however, did not follow immediately, is evident from the next statement. "The people of the prince [or 'ruler'] that shall come [not Messiah, for He had already come, and been cut off] shall destroy the city and the sanctuary [fulfilled when the Roman armies destroyed the temple and later the city, in 70 A.D. and 135 A.D., respectively], and the end thereof shall be with a flood [literally 'overflowing,' fulfilled in the worldwide dispersion of the Jews, when they flowed out of Judah, as it were, into all nations], and unto the end of the war, desolations are determined [that is, 'wars and desolations are determined until the end']."

This also has been fulfilled, not only in the destruction of Jerusalem and the dispersion of its people, but also in the fact that wars and desolations have continued almost without pause in the world ever since. This prediction, in fact, leaps over all the centuries right to the times of "the end." It is then that finally the seventieth seven-years "are determined upon thy people." Here is what will happen then:

> *And he [that is, 'the ruler that shall come'] shall confirm the covenant with many for one week: and in the midst of the week he shall cause the sacrifice and the oblation to cease, and for the overspreading of abominations he shall make it desolate, even until the consummation, ...*
> *(Daniel 9:27)*

There will, therefore, be a treaty made by the coming ruler with the Jewish people and their leaders, permitting them finally to reclaim that part of Jerusalem still controlled by the Muslims, to raze the Dome of the Rock, to build their temple there on the sacred site, and reestablish their ancient worship. The treaty will be for a seven-year period, but at the midpoint of that period, the ruler will call an abrupt halt to their sacrifices and oblations, thus breaking the treaty. Note that, in order to halt these rituals, they must have been previously inaugurated, the context thus making it clear that this was the essence of the treaty itself. This, in turn, has to mean that the Jews by this time have returned from their dispersion and have established a formal government capable of making and implementing a treaty. This situation exists today, and is, as we have seen, a sure sign of the time of the end. Further, this implies that the Muslim influence there has been eliminated (as discussed in Chapter 2), and that a new power, centered in western Europe, will have become strong enough to initiate such a treaty. These developments have been noted in Chapter 4.

The reason the ruler will break the treaty is for "the overspreading of abominations." As we have noted before, the term "abominations" refers especially to idol worship. The word for "overspreading" conveys the idea of "extremity" or "uttermost extent." In other words, this ungodly ruler will decide to replace the Jewish temple worship of the Creator with the most extreme type of idolatry. By this time, he will have so consolidated his control of his alliance of the western nations that he can undertake the elimination of all recognition of the true God and require that men give all honor and obeisance to him alone. He will set up a gigantic statue of himself (supposedly representing all mankind) in the temple, and require that all worship henceforth be directed there. Those who refuse—especially the Jews whose temple he has desecrated—will be executed.

This terrible act of blasphemy will be "desolating" (or "stupefying") to the Jews and to all others who still believe in God. That this will actually happen is confirmed by Paul, who also further identifies this "prince that shall come." He writes of the coming "day of Christ," or "the day of the Lord" when

> ... that man of sin (will) be revealed, the son of perdition, Who opposeth and exalteth himself above all that is called God, or that is worshiped; so that he as God sitteth in the temple of God, shewing himself that he is God (II Thessalonians 2:3,4).

The Lord Jesus Christ Himself clearly confirmed this interpretation of Daniel's prophecy, with the following warning:

> When ye therefore shall see the abomination of desolation, spoken of by Daniel the prophet, stand in the holy place, ... Then let them which be in Judea flee into the mountains; ... For then shall be great tribulation, such as was not since the beginning of the world to this time, no, nor ever shall be (Matthew 24:15,16,21).

As we have seen in Chapter 3, this will be "the time of Jacob's trouble" (Jeremiah 30:7). It will be at greatest intensity during the 3½ years comprising the last half of Daniel's seventieth week. It will be so terrible that Jesus said: "Except those days should be shortened, there should no flesh be saved" (Matthew 24:22). The world could not endure a much longer such time than 3½ years.

This same period was mentioned also by the angel who had already spoken to Daniel about the great Beast who was going to gain dominion for a brief period in the last days:

> *And he shall speak great words against the most*
> *High, and shall wear out the saints of the most*
> *High, and think to change times and laws: and*
> *they shall be given into his hand until a time and*
> *times and the dividing of time (Daniel 7:25).*

The same period is mentioned also in Daniel 12:7.

The last book of the Bible is largely occupied with the events of Daniel's seventieth week, in Chapters 6 through 19. The period of 1260 days (that is 3½ years of 360 days each) is mentioned as the period of ministry of the two witnesses (Revelation 11:3), before the Beast finally kills them, after which he will rule the world for 42 months (Revelation 13:5). This also is 3½ years, the two periods thus adding to the whole seven years.

The Two Witnesses

The detailed events that will take place during this last seven years of the present age are given in the book of Revelation, which in turn draws upon, clarifies and completes all the previous prophecies dealing with this period, as given in both Old and New Testaments. I believe the book of Revelation should be taken literally (except, of course, when its own context indicates otherwise—in which case the Bible itself makes clear the meaning of its figures of speech, so that the reader need not depend on his own imagination). For those wanting a verse-by-verse exposition of this climactic book of the Bible, using this approach, please see my detailed commentary, *The Revelation Record* (Tyndale, 1983, 521 pp.).

The first 3½-year period is described in Revelation Chapters 6 through 9, the second 3½ years in Chapters 16 through 19. The central chapters, 10 through 15, are parenthetical, seen from the perspective of the midpoint of the seven-year period, but also looking back through history to the very beginning of creation, and forward to the ages of the eternal future.

From the time God created the world and gave Adam and Eve dominion over it until he called Abraham to found a new nation, He was dealing with the entire world of mankind and, after Babel, with all its nations. From Abraham to Christ, He was dealing especially with Israel. Each of these periods seems to have occupied about 2000 years. Both groups rebelled against their Creator, and God sent prophet after prophet to call them back, but they failed. After Christ, God left the nations—both Jews and Gentiles—to their own devices, as it were, calling out His Church (saved individuals, whether Jew or Gentile) as a "people for His name" (Acts 15:14), and this has gone on for almost another 2000 years.

√ At roughly the midpoint of the pre-Jewish (Gentile) dispensation lived a great prophet named Enoch, who preached against the wickedness of his own day and prophesied of the coming judgment (Jude 14-15). Similarly, at roughly the midpoint of the Israel dispensation, a great prophet named Elijah prophesied against the wickedness of Israel. It is noteworthy that these two prophets, representing God's prophetic ministry to both the world at large and to Israel in particular, were translated into heaven in the very midst of their ministries, as it were, going directly into heaven without dying, still in their physical bodies, the only two men in all history who were so privileged (note Genesis 5:23-24; Hebrews 11:5; II Kings 2:11).

It was as though God wanted to preserve them in heaven in order to send them back to complete their ministries in a future day. God is not capricious and it is difficult to perceive any other reason why these two men—alone out of all God's great witnesses throughout the ages—would be so favored.

In fact, we know this is why Elijah was called up. The very last words of the Old Testament—God's last prophetic message to Israel before the coming of Christ—were these: "Behold, I will send you Elijah the prophet before the coming of the great and dreadful day of the LORD: And he shall turn the heart of the fathers to the children, and the heart of the children to their fathers, lest I come and smite the earth with a curse" (Malachi 4:5,6). Jesus also said: "Elias truly shall first come, and restore all things" (Matthew 17:11). Jesus (before He came into the world) had seen Elijah waiting there in heaven for this future ministry! In one sense, John the Baptist had come "in the spirit and power of Elias" (Luke 1:17), but he himself recognized that he was not really Elijah (John 1:21).

There can be no reasonable doubt, therefore, that Elijah's "sending" is fulfilled when God says: "I will give power unto my two witnesses, and they shall prophesy a thousand, two hundred and threescore days" (Revelation 11:3). The second witness, almost as certainly, must be Enoch, for he must finish his prophecy to the Gentile world just as Elijah must finish his to Israel. Their power will include the ability "to smite the earth with all plagues," and they will be invulnerable until the Beast is finally able to kill them (Revelation 11:5-7). This accomplishment—finally ridding the earth of "these two prophets (who) tormented them that dwelt on the earth" (Revelation 11:10), will enable the Beast to complete and consolidate his rule over the earth, and "to continue forty and two months" (Revelation 13:5).

Thus, the prophetic and warning ministry of God's two end-time witnesses will clearly be during the first half of Daniel's seventieth "week," followed by the unlimited rule of the Beast during the last half.

Now, although the last half will be "the great tribulation," as Christ called it (Matthew 24:21), and "the time of Jacob's trouble" (Jeremiah 30:7), the first half will also be a time of severe divine judgment on the earth. The two witnesses will be calling down great plagues on the earth—such things as wars, famines, pestilences and earthquakes, then later hail, fire, meteorite bombardments, and great darkness, finally even hordes of deadly demonic creatures from the pit of Hades—all seeking to warn men to flee from the wrath to come. No wonder those on the earth will rejoice when the Beast overcomes them! This is not mere human persecution of other humans, as some have viewed the tribulation period, but the outpouring of God's wrath on an ungodly world, called down by Enoch and Elijah.

From a human perspective, the two witnesses will be considered by the people as responsible for their torments. Actually, the plagues will have been sent from heaven, as the Lamb breaks the seals on the great scroll representing His ownership of the earth (Revelation 6) and His angels sound their successive trumpets (Revelation 8 and 9). In fact, no doubt because this will be the theme of the prophetic preaching of the two witnesses, many men will acknowledge that the Lamb is on His throne and that "the great day of His wrath is come" (Revelation 6:17), but they will not repent "of the works of their hands, that they should not worship devils, and idols ... Neither repented they of their murders, nor of their sorceries [that is, use of drugs], nor of their fornication, nor of their thefts" (Revelation 9:20–21).

Although most people will reject their testimony, there will no doubt be a goodly number who will believe and be saved, thereby calling down on themselves persecution by those who have firmly committed their souls to the evolutionary pantheism of the widely promoted world religion of "Mystery

Babylon," as discussed in Chapter 4. One such fruit of their testimony will apparently be the 144,000 Israeli witnesses described in Revelation 7:4-8. These will continue to proclaim their own testimony after the two prophets are gone, especially to their Jewish brethren, thus preparing their whole nation to receive Christ when He finally returns in glory.

In addition, there will be "a great multitude ... of all nations, and kindreds, and people, and tongues ... which came out of (the) great tribulation" (Revelation 7:9,14). Perhaps these will be won by the two witnesses, or by the 144,000, or by reading Bibles or Christian books, or by the angel who will later be preaching the gospel from the sky (Revelation 14:6,7), but in any case there will be many saved during this coming time of judgment.

Finally, God's two witnesses will be slain. Enoch and Elijah have lived in mortal bodies without dying for thousands of years, but finally they (as have so many prophets before) must also be martyred. Then, in beautiful irony, after 3½ days (reminding men of the 3½ years of their witness), they will be raised from the dead and raptured back into heaven, for the eyes of all to see (Revelation 11:9,12), no doubt via world-wide television.

Image of the Beast

Just before the two witnesses are described, there is a brief reference to the new temple in Jerusalem (Revelation 11:1,2). As noted before, the treaty made with the Jews at the beginning of the seven years, by the ruler called the Beast, will allow them to build their temple and restore their worship. There have been unconfirmed rumors that materials for the temple are being prepared today, and it is known that at least one sect of Orthodox Jews has been advocating this for years. In any case, it is likely that the temple will be finished very quickly once construction begins. Possibly the presence of Elijah during this period, "turning the hearts of the children to the fathers" could be a key factor in this project.

But then, as we have noted both from Daniel and Christ's Olivet Discourse, after 3½ years, the Beast will break his treaty with the Jews and "the holy city shall they tread under foot forty and two months," (Revelation 11:2), which is the 3½ year period during which the Beast will exercise global power (Revelation 13:5-7). This is when the "abomination of desolation" will be set up in the holy place of the temple, and the terrible persecution of the Jews, along with any Christian believers who refuse to worship the image of the Beast, will begin.

More information is given about this image in Revelation 13. This is another of the parenthetical chapters in Revelation, given from the vantage point of the middle of the seven years, but also looking back to the very beginning, when Satan first rebelled against God. In Revelation 12, he is introduced under the symbol of a great red dragon, about to attack a symbolic woman in the heavens who was ready to deliver a man-child (Revelation 12:1-4). This is undoubtedly referring in figure to the primeval prophecy of the future conflict between the seed of the woman and the seed of the serpent (Genesis 3:15). The former is Christ, the "man-child, who was to rule all nations with a rod of iron" (Revelation 12:5; compare Revelation 19:15). The seed of the serpent is the Beast, called "the son of perdition" (II Thessalonians 2:3), who (as the dragon) is described as "having seven heads and ten horns" (Revelation 12:3; 13:1).

The dragon and his angels (one-third of the stars of heaven [the stars symbolizing angels—note Revelation 12:4,9])— were unsuccessful, however, for the man-child was caught up unto God (verse 5), and the dragon and his angels (apparently just at this midpoint of the seven-year period) will be permanently cast out from any further access to heaven (12:7–8).

That there can be no question as to the reality behind the symbolic dragon, John tells us that "the great dragon was cast out, that old serpent, called the Devil, and Satan, which deceiveth the whole world" (Revelation 12:9). The latter phrase is especially significant, for it reminds us that Satan's lie has deceived all nations of the world, past and present. The essence of that lie, of course, is his evolutionary explanation for all things, denying that God is Creator and alleging that all things have evolved somehow from the primeval watery chaos. Thus, the true God can be ignored, so the lie goes on to say, and Man can be worshiped as "God." Man is the pinnacle of all past evolutionary processes, and this greatest of all men will require that he be worshiped as the representative of all men.

To accomplish this, his "minister of religion," whom John describes as "another beast" (Revelation 13:7), will issue a decree that the first Beast must be worshiped by all people. To this end, he will erect a giant image of the Beast (the "abomination of desolation"), and have it set up in the temple at Jerusalem. Furthermore, "he had power to give life to the image," so that "as many as would not worship the image" would be put to death (Revelation 13:15).

The technology is practically at hand already for all this to be accomplished scientifically. The sciences of robotics, holography, video-communication, laser weaponry, and super-computers, among others, are so developed that one can easily visualize small models of the great image in every home, monitored by a control center at the headquarters of this "false prophet," activating some lethal device if any specified act of worship is not properly performed. Dissent cannot be tolerated if perfect "peace and harmony" are to be maintained. Further control will be assured by requiring a "mark" to be imprinted on the right hand or forehead of all who would buy or sell (Revelation 13:17), perhaps one that is visible only under an electrical or optical scanner.

The "life" which is given to the image can hardly be real life, however, since only God is the Creator, and conscious life—even of animals—is a special creation (Genesis 1:21). Nevertheless, "he doeth great wonders" (Revelation 13:13), which no doubt are "lying wonders" (note Matthew 24:24;

II Thessalonians 2:9), capable of deceiving men into believing that he, indeed, is all-powerful. The deception will be more convincing than a robot with computerized brain and automated bodily motion would be, for these already are becoming common, but he could not create real bodily life. In any case, the deception will be effective, for "all that dwell upon the earth will worship him, whose names are not written in the Book of Life of the Lamb slain from the foundation of the world" (Revelation 13:8).

This tells us, though, that there will be some—perhaps many—whose names are written in the Book of Life, and so will refuse the mark. They will be hunted and executed if they are caught, but some will survive, perhaps by hiding, drawing on their food reserves, living off the land, or whatever. Even execution, however, will be far preferable to the fate of all who agree to receive the mark of the beast, for "the smoke of their torment ascendeth up forever and ever" (Revelation 14:11).

Those who do come "out of (the) great tribulation" without compromise, on the other hand, "shall hunger no more, neither thirst any more," for "God shall wipe away all tears from their eyes" (Revelation 7:14,16,17).

The Woman in the Wilderness

There is yet another reference to the last 3½ years in Revelation—in fact, two separate references to the same event.

And the woman fled into the wilderness, where she hath a place prepared of God, that they should feed her there a thousand two hundred and threescore days.

And to the woman were given two wings of a great eagle, that she might fly into the wilderness, into her place, where she is nourished for a time, and times, and half a time, from the face of the serpent. (Revelation 12:6,14)

The "woman" is the one who has given birth to the "man-child" (verse 5), the promised Seed, slain by the "dragon" but resurrected and caught up to God's throne. While Mary was the actual mother of Christ, the above verses obviously must refer not to His biological mother, but to His national mother, the nation of Israel, recognized in the Old Testament as the "wife of Jehovah."

When the image of the Beast, the "abomination of desolation" is set up in the holy place in Jerusalem, Jewish believers in God will be in grave jeopardy, and will have to flee quickly for their lives. In his sermon on the Mount of Olives, the Lord Jesus had warned them long ago to "flee unto the mountains," without even bothering to retrieve any of their possessions (Matthew 24:16–18), for this would be the sign that the great tribulation was under way.

The wilderness and the mountains of which these Scriptures speak are probably in the area of modern Jordan southeast of the Dead Sea, in the ancient countries of Edom, Moab and Ammon. There, many of the people of Israel, those who are able to escape the armies of the Beast, forced to flee from their temple and its revived worship of Jehovah, very likely accompanied by at least some of the already converted 144,000 witnesses, will spend 3½ years learning about Christ. There they will be providentially protected and nourished, just as their ancestors, 3500 years before, had been preserved and prepared in the wilderness for their entrance into the promised land.

Come, my people, enter into thy chambers, and shut thy doors about thee: hide thyself as it were for a little moment, until the indignation be overpast. For, behold, the LORD cometh out of His place to punish the inhabitants of the earth for their iniquity (Isaiah 26:20,21).

Therefore, behold, I will ... bring her into the wilderness, and speak comfortably unto her, ... and I will say to them which were not my people, Thou art my people; and they shall say, Thou art my God (Hosea 2:14,23).

The dragon, that old serpent, will seek to kill the woman, no doubt using the Beast and his armies, sent forth in great waves to overwhelm the people of God. But "when the enemy shall come in like a flood, the Spirit of the LORD shall lift up a standard against him" (Isaiah 59:19). A great fissure will open in the earth and swallow the pursuing armies (Revelation 12:16).

There will also be other Jews all over the world who are affected by these events, as well as new Christian believers in every tribe and nation, who will refuse the mark of the Beast and will, if they can escape the death squads, have to flee for their lives, also. They cannot escape into the mountains and wilderness of Judaea, as do those in Jerusalem and other parts of Israel, but they can still follow the advice of Christ and flee into the mountains of their own lands. Although many may be caught and put to death, there will be at least some who will survive the entire 3½ years of great tribulation, ready to meet the Lord following His return in glory at the coming battle of Armageddon.

When Satan and his Man of Sin find they cannot reach those who are being supernaturally protected in the wilderness areas of Jordan, they will intensify their efforts to destroy all others everywhere who will not worship the image of the Beast.

> *And the dragon was wroth with the woman, and went to make war with the remnant of her seed, which keep the commandments of God, and have the testimony of Jesus Christ (Revelation 12:17).*

The conflict between the "seed of the serpent" and the "seed of the woman" thus will continue right on to the end. The armies and police forces of the Beast (all of whom, spiritually, are "cursed children" of the Serpent) will search the whole world to find and destroy, if they can, all those who remain of the spiritual seed of the Woman.

Who is the Antichrist?

Ever since the Apostolic Period, Christians seem to have been fascinated by the prophecies concerning Antichrist— also called the Beast, the Man of Sin and other such unsavory names in the Scriptures. In the first century, many of the persecuted saints thought (naturally enough) that the Emperor Nero was the Antichrist, and there have been many other nominees since. During and after the Reformation Period, many Protestant leaders argued that the Pope, with his Roman Church, was the Antichrist. At the same time, Catholics taught that Martin Luther and the Protestants in general constituted the Antichrist, with Mystery Babylon being Jerusalem.

At various times in history, others have been proposed for this position—Napoleon, Hitler, etc.—but none so far have really conformed to the various Biblical descriptions of Antichrist. For many years, Benito Mussolini, as Italy's dictator with ambitions to restore Rome's ancient empire, was considered to be a prime candidate. The most recent leader touted for the position has been Saddam Hussein. All of these men hated Christ and his Word, and presumably should be included among the "many antichrists" noted by the Apostle John (I John 2:18), but none were the Antichrist. The fact is that his identity has not yet been revealed.

The event that should clearly reveal his identity, as we have noted from Daniel's prophecy of the seventy weeks, is when a great and charismatic ruler is able to make a seven-year covenant with the nation of Israel, allowing them to rebuild their temple and reestablish their ancient worship (Daniel 9:27). For him to be able to do this, he must already have been able to achieve a position of great prominence and authority among the nations of the West, but the seven-year treaty with Israel will make it certain that he is the one. He will then spend the next 3½ years consolidating and enlarging his power. Then, as we have seen, he will break the treaty with Israel, setting up his own image—the "abomination of desolation"—in their temple at Jerusalem, "so that he as God sitteth in the temple of God, shewing himself that he is God" (II Thessalonians 2:4).

He is not yet able to do any of this, however, because there is someone restraining him, and that person must first "be taken out of the way. And then shall that Wicked (One) be revealed" (II Thessalonians 2:7,8). No wonder we cannot yet identify him!

But who can restrain such a man from doing what he desires? For he it is "whose coming is after the working of Satan with all power and signs and lying wonders" (II Thessalonians 2:9). No one can restrain Satan but God, but how can God be taken out of the way? Somehow, the presence and power of God must be removed from the world before the presence and power of Satan and his Satan-possessed Man of Sin can be at liberty to fully implement their plans for the world.

God is now immediately present in the world, of course, only in the person of His Holy Spirit, who is Himself abiding in every true believer in the Lord Jesus Christ. Thus, for the Holy Spirit to "be taken out of the way," all true believers would have to be taken out of the way as well. It is their presence in the world, indwelt and empowered by the Holy Spirit, that is hindering the revealing of the Antichrist!

This is also implied in verse 3. "For that day shall not come (i.e., the day of the Lord, or the beginning of the seven-year tribulation period), except there come a falling away first, and that Man of Sin be revealed, the Son of perdition." Evidently the "falling away" and the "taking out of the way" are simultaneous, if not identical, events, since the revealing of the Wicked One immediately follows in each case.

The Greek word translated "falling away" is *apostasia*, meaning literally "standing apart" or "separation." It is used only twice in the New Testament, being translated "forsake" in its other occurrence. It could easily be understood as synonymous to "taking out of the way." Because it can be transliterated as "apostasy," however, it is commonly understood by expositors as the apostasy of Christian churches just before the revealing of the Man of Sin.

There are two problems with this interpretation. First, there have been so many periods of apostasy in the professing church, ever since the apostolic period, that the only way an apostasy mentioned here could have any special significance would be for it to be so universal as to affect the entire Christian church. This would practically amount to the same thing as for the entire church to "be taken out of the way."

Secondly, the "falling away" was an event about which the Thessalonian believers already had been instructed (note verse 5), but there is no previous mention of a religious apostasy in either of the Thessalonian epistles. There is, however, in I Thessalonians 4:13–17, the most definitive presentation in all the Bible of the doctrine of the "catching away" of both dead and living believers out of the world to be with Christ. If the "falling away" is understood as referring to this event, translating *apostasia* as, say, "separating," then the apparent connection with the "taking away" referred to in verse 7 becomes quite clear. Both are pointing to the fact that the Antichrist will not be revealed until all genuine Christian believers in this present age are taken out of the world to be with Christ. This great event will be discussed more fully in Chapter 7. It needs to be mentioned at this point in order to stress that no one now can determine who the Antichrist will be, even though it is likely that he is some man now living and being prepared by Satan for his revealing.

Now, although we cannot determine his identity at this time, the Bible does indicate a number of his characteristics. In the first place, the seventy weeks prophecy tells us that his nationality will be that of the "people" (Daniel 9:26) who destroyed the Jewish temple in 70 A.D., and the city in 135 A.D. This might identify him as an Italian (one reason why Mussolini was believed by so many in the 1920's and 1930's to be the future Antichrist), but this is not necessarily the case. There is some evidence that the "Roman" army that destroyed Jerusalem consisted largely of Syrian conscripts.

It is even possible that it could mean someone from one of the many nations in the old Roman empire, or even in the "extended" or "revised" Roman empire of the last days. There are also references to "the Assyrian" in certain Old Testament latter-day prophecies that suggest the Antichrist (see Isaiah 10; 24; 30:31).

In fact, the great prophecy of Christ's birth in Bethlehem (Micah 5:2) goes on to say that this coming "ruler in Israel; whose goings forth have been from of old, from everlasting" will eventually "be great unto the ends of the earth" and that His armies will waste "the land of Nimrod" and "deliver us from the Assyrian, when he cometh into our land" (Micah 5:4,6).

Here is another reference to Babel, "the land of Nimrod" in the last days, suggesting that its king, "the Assyrian," has wrongfully "come into our land." Nimrod was founder of both Babel and Nineveh (the capital of Assyria), and Babylonia, Assyria and Syria were all interconnected both geographically and politically. This indicates at least the possibility that Antichrist will either come from this region, or else will be called the "the Assyrian" because he has made Babylon his capital, as discussed in Chapter 4. All of this leaves the national origin of the Beast still uncertain, except that he will not come from South Africa or East Asia!

There are certain other characteristics of Antichrist that are described in the prophetic Scriptures. He will be a pantheistic evolutionist, as well as supremely egotistic, though he comes from a God-fearing family background.

And the king shall do according to his will; and he shall exalt himself, and magnify himself above every god, and shall speak marvelous things against the God of gods, ... Neither shall he regard the God of his fathers, nor the desire of women, nor regard any god: for he shall magnify himself above all. But in his estate shall he honor the God of forces (Daniel 11:36-38).

The word for "forces" here is often translated "strength" or "fortress." Instead of the true God, this man will worship a nature god personifying strength and power.

He will also exhibit brilliant ability to bring peace and prosperity to those nations that willingly yield to his sovereignty.

And in the latter time of their kingdom, when the transgressors are come to the full, a king of fierce countenance, and understanding dark sentences, shall stand up. And his power shall be mighty, but not by his own power: and he shall destroy wonderfully, and shall prosper, and practice, and shall destroy the mighty and the holy people. And through his policy also he shall cause craft to prosper in his hand,—and he shall magnify himself in his heart, and by peace shall destroy many: he shall also stand up against the Prince of princes; but he shall be broken without hand (Daniel 8:23-25).

There is, of course, another enigmatic clue as to the identity of the Beast—a clue seemingly given for the purpose of recognizing him before his official "revealing."

> *Here is wisdom. Let him that hath understanding count the number of the Beast: for it is the number of a man; and his number is six hundred threescore and six (Revelation 13:18).*

This nugget of divinely given wisdom assures us that the Beast is a man, not some movement or institution. Furthermore, it is clearly referring to the "numerical equivalent" of this man's name, or title, or both.

In the language of the New Testament writings, each Greek letter was also used as a number (the letter alpha indicated "one," beta "two," gamma "three," and so on). This was unlike our English language, which uses different symbols (the Arabic numerals) to indicate numbers.

Thus, to "count the number" of any Greek word, one simply added the number values of all the letters in the word. How to apply this procedure to a modern name, however, is uncertain.

One possibility would be to transliterate the name into the New Testament Greek alphabet, and then add its numbers. For example, the English word "bag" would be "beta-alpha-gamma" in Greek, with a numerical value of $2 + 1 + 3$, or 6.

Another possibility would be to assign a number to each letter in the appropriate modern language, using the same approach the Greeks used ($A = 1$, $B = 2$, $C = 3$, etc.), and then count up the numerical value of the person's name in his own language. This procedure is at least as questionable as the first. Perhaps there is some better approach, but it is obvious that this is not as yet a clearly formulated procedure. Probably it will become more clear by the time people really need to know the number of the name of the Beast. That time is not yet, however, and for the present, his identity remains unrevealed.

In any case, his reign will be brief—a mere seven years. But they will be seven years of fury. He will have finally achieved the age-long goal of all evolutionary humanistic pantheists—a world government, with a worldwide economy and worldwide culture, all centered in and controlled by "the creature rather than the Creator" (Romans 1:25)—and he will be furious with those who will not submit, seeking to destroy them all if he can. More than that, however, these seven years will be years of divine fury—"the great and the terrible day of the LORD" (Joel 2:31). These earth-changing judgments from God are outlined in the next chapter.

CHAPTER 6

Science and the Second Coming

The Groaning Creation

When God finished His work of "creating and making" all things in the six days of Creation Week, He surveyed everything He had done and pronounced it all "very good!" (Genesis 1:31). With the entrance of sin into the world, however, God had to impose the judgment of decay and death upon Adam and all his dominion. "Cursed is the ground for thy sake," He said to Adam (Genesis 3:17). The very dust of the ground (the basic elements out of which all material systems had been made, including even the body of Adam) was thus brought under what the Apostle Paul called "the bondage of corruption (literally 'decay')" (Romans 8:21). Under the curse, "the whole creation groaneth and travaileth in pain together until now" (Romans 8:22). "Of old hast thou laid the foundation of the earth: and the heavens are the work of thy hands ... yea, all of them shall wax old, like a garment: ... and they shall be changed" (Psalm 102:25-26).

This principle is so universal that scientists have come to recognize it as a basic law of science, calling it the law of increasing entropy" or "the second law of thermodynamics." They generally refuse, however, to acknowledge its Biblical basis and its theological significance.

Furthermore, they reject its obvious testimony against their belief in universal evolution. The fact is, nevertheless, that the world is not progressing upward through an imaginary process of evolution, but downward toward disintegration and death, by the very real processes of thermodynamics.

This decay principle has always operated in the world, but now seems to be rapidly accelerating. As noted in the first chapter, one of the signs of the last days is an explosive increase in science and technology. It is ironic that these amazing scientific discoveries and technological inventions seem themselves to be hastening these decay processes. The whole world seems to be sick and dying.

Even without the witness of the prophetic Scriptures, we can know we are in the last days of Planet Earth, for it simply cannot survive much longer apart from divine intervention. The world's leaders and planners need to consider all of these modern secular "signs" in light of both God's primeval Curse and His coming judgment on man's rebellion. It is not necessary to document these developments here, for they are all well-known and thoroughly documented in secular scientific literature. It will be instructive, however, merely to list and comment very briefly on some of them. Each is ominous enough by itself but, when compiled together, they surely constitute massive evidence that the world cannot last much longer, if Christ does not return. One could predict that, if He doesn't come soon, there will be nothing left to come to! Some of these fearful signs are listed below.

(1) *Global water pollution.* The earth is the only "water planet," and water is absolutely essential for life, but its lakes and rivers—even its oceans—are rapidly being poisoned by sewage, toxic wastes and other forms of pollution.

(2) *Global air pollution.* Not only are the earth's cities becoming enveloped in noxious smog, but its atmosphere is being contaminated with carbon dioxide from fossil fuels (most recently by the burning of Kuwaiti oil fields), fluorocarbons that are destroying its protective ozone layer, and other contaminants that affect both its greenhouse gases and normal precipitation.

(3) *Population explosion.* Although much of its surface is still uninhabited, Earth's population—especially in under-developed countries—is outstripping food supplies, and famines are increasing.

(4) *Incurable pestilences.* The dread disease of AIDS, apparently incurable and always lethal, is spreading so rapidly as to threaten the very existence of mankind. Despite modern medical advances, many other diseases are spreading, and even epidemic diseases once believed conquered (tuberculosis, malaria, smallpox,

bubonic plague and others) are returning in virulent strains.

(5) *Sophisticated weapons of destruction.* Many nations are acquiring nuclear weapons now, in addition to terrifying biological and chemical agents, laser weapons, electro-magnetic devices of unimagined potential, psychic warfare machines, neutron bombs, and other exotic lethal devices which could destroy all life on earth if unleashed and unrestrained.

(6) *Soil erosion.* The planet's very thin layer of topsoil, so necessary for agriculture and food production, is being lost through irrigation, urbanization, deforestation and other carelessness. Many once-productive regions are now deserts.

(7) *Destruction of rain forests.* The Amazon jungles and other rain forests of the earth are rapidly being cleared for various ephemeral human uses, affecting the earth's very fragile ecological balance and its vital food chains.

(8) *Explosive increase of drug use.* In America especially, but other nations also, the entire younger generation is in danger of being lost to useful society, or even to life itself, by the unprecedented proliferation of drug addiction.

(9) *Legalized abortion and homosexuality.* The unthinkable (only a generation ago) legalization of abortion and homosexual practice—and their promotion as preferred lifestyles—with all forms of sexual

promiscuity, could, if allowed to continue to grow unchecked, eventually eliminate future generations.

(10) *Species extinctions.* It is known that at least one (more likely three or four) species of plant or animal life is becoming extinct every day, and this has been happening every day throughout human history. This very fact is a strong indictment against evolution, for no new species are known to have evolved in this period. However, all kinds were created by God for specific purposes, and their loss is harmful to the whole global ecology. At the same time, many dangerous species of bacteria, insects, etc., are proliferating as a result.

(11) *Chemical pollution.* In addition to chemicals polluting the air and water, there are many other deadly substances threatening life. Pesticides, food additives, over-the-counter drugs, insecticides, nuclear wastes and other chemicals—many of them carcinogenic or harmful to human health in numerous other ways—are increasingly endangering the global environment and life on earth.

Any one of the above modern developments, among others that could be mentioned, might be able to destroy all life on earth if allowed to continue unchecked. Each one is a direct result of the sinful nature of man and his refusal to regard his divinely given dominion over the earth (Genesis 1:26–28) as a responsible stewardship from God. Instead, he has been a despoiler of the earth and his fellow man, and this is one reason why God is coming soon to set things right. "For behold, the Lord cometh out of His place to punish the inhabitants of the earth for their iniquity" (Isaiah 26:21). In that great day of His wrath, He will "destroy them which destroy the earth" (Revelation 11:18).

The iniquity of the earth's inhabitants goes far beyond abusing their responsibilities to the earth, of course. "For as it was in the days of Noah," Christ said, "so shall it be also in the days of the Son of man" (Luke 17:26). In those days, after a period of patient longsuffering on God's part, "the flood came, and destroyed them all." In the days of Noah, as fast coming true again in these last days, "God saw that the wickedness of man was great in the earth" and that "all flesh had corrupted his way upon the earth" (Genesis 6:5,12).

Crime, cruelty, war, immorality, dishonesty, drunkenness and other gross sins of the flesh abound today all over the world. Even those who live more or less honest, moral, kindly lives, however, have in most cases broken God's first commandment, when He said: "Thou shalt have no other gods before me" (Exodus 20:3). Atheism, pantheism, humanism, liberalism, legalism, occultism and other false religions abound among "good" people and—in the view of the God of power, holiness and sacrificial love—this may be the greatest sin of all.

The Lost World and the World to Come

God cannot fail, and He created this world and its inhabitants for a glorious and eternal purpose. Sin and the Curse have intervened for a little season, but He has promised someday to "make all things new" again (Revelation 21:5). "I know that, whatsoever God doeth, it shall be for ever; nothing can be put to it, nor anything taken from it: and God doeth it, that men should fear before him" (Ecclesiastes 3:14). Eventually, the earth will be purified, the Curse removed, and everything will again be "very good" (Genesis 1:31), as it was in the beginning.

But all this will not be done overnight. Before the new earth is prepared for eternity, there will first be the seven-year period of tribulation on the earth, then a thousand-year period when Christ and the saints reign on this earth (Revelation 20:1-6). There seems no substantial reason not to take this revelation literally. The "thousand-year" period is mentioned *explicitly* no less than six times (Revelation 20:2-7).

God, in His Word, has given us some thrilling insights concerning the changes that will be occurring in the earth during these periods, and it is instructive to note the remarkable parallels and contrasts along a time line between old and new—between the lost world of Adam and the people before the great flood, and the new world of Christ and His saints.

The primeval world of Eden was a "very good" world, with no sin, no suffering, no death, no curse. Similarly, in the new earth, "God shall wipe away all tears from their eyes; and there shall be no more death, neither sorrow, nor crying, neither shall there be any more pain: ... And there shall be no more curse:" (Revelation 21:4; 22:3).

Since the Curse now permeates the very elements of the earth, its removal requires purging the elements. This, indeed, is what will happen: "The elements shall melt with fervent heat, the earth also and the works that are therein shall be burned up ... all these things shall be dissolved" (II Peter 3:10,11). They will not be annihilated, of course, for "whatsoever God doeth, it shall be for ever!" (Ecclesiastes 3:14). His law of conservation stipulates that one state of matter can be converted into another, and even matter itself can be converted into energy. The chemical energy locked in the dust of the earth will be converted into heat and light and sound energy—"the heavens shall pass away with a great noise, and ... fervent heat ... being on fire."— but it will not be annihilated. With His creative Word, God will convert the purified energy again into the material substance of the earth and its atmospheric heaven. "For, behold, I create new heavens and a new earth" (Isaiah 65:17).

For the Curse and death to be removed, sin must also be forever banished. Therefore we, "according to His promise, look for new heavens and a new earth, wherein dwelleth righteousness." (II Peter 3:13). By that time, all the children of God, redeemed through faith in Christ, will have been "conformed to the image of His Son" (Romans 8:29), with resurrected bodies and the very mind of Christ. Thus will the new earth and its inhabitants at last be restored to the conditions of the Edenic earth, except that the very possibility of sin will vanish, along with all reminders of past sin and judgment (e.g., the great fossil beds).

In the same way, the earth just after the Curse was imposed on it (i.e., the earth before the great flood, the antediluvian earth) is parallel in many ways to the earth just before the Curse is removed (i.e., the earth during the 1000-year reign of Christ, the millennial earth). When God cursed the ground after Adam's sin, the principle of death and decay immediately began to operate, but outwardly the world still looked much the same: a beautiful, pleasant, "very good" world, with abundant provision of all needs for human and animal life.

Similarly, the millennial world, where Christ and His redeemed saints will reign for a thousand years, will again be a beautiful world of peace and prosperity, a world where war and crime and overt sin will not be allowed at all. Yet people will still be born in the flesh, with their inherited sin natures, and will still be sinful inwardly, even if not outwardly, until they (just as people in every age) are born again spiritually through faith in the redemptive work of God, in Christ, on their behalf. Furthermore, there will still be death during the millennium. People will live hundreds of years again, just as their counterparts did in the antediluvian period, but they will still be subject to death.

There shall be no more thence an infant of days, nor an old man that hath not filled his days; for the child shall die an hundred years old; but the sinner being an hundred years old shall be accursed (Isaiah 65:20).

Apparently, there will be a reversion even in the animal world from predation and carnivorous appetites back to the harmony and herbivorous behavior of the primeval animal environment.

> *The wolf also shall dwell with the lamb, and the leopard shall lie down with the kid; and the calf and the young lion and the fatling together; and a little child shall lead them. And the cow and the bear shall feed; their young ones shall lie down together: and the lion shall eat straw like the ox .... They shall not hurt nor destroy in all my holy mountain: for the earth shall be full of the knowledge of the Lord, as the waters cover the sea: (Isaiah 11:6,7,9).*

The earth itself will be restored largely in the millennium to its antediluvian beauty. In the original "very good" creation, there were no uninhabitable deserts or ice caps or high mountains. The seas were relatively narrow and shallow, all inter-connected and more or less uniformly distributed among the earth's land surfaces, thus assuring a relatively equable humidity everywhere.

In the original creation, "the Lord God had not caused it to rain upon the earth, ... But there went up a mist from the earth, and watered the whole face of the ground" (Genesis 2:5,6). There was no change in this regime until the great flood, when rain came in torrents from the skies for forty days and forty nights. When the rains ceased, the rainbow appeared in the sky for the first time in history (Genesis 7:12; 9:13).

Many of the above phenomena can be explained by the "waters above the firmament" (Genesis 1:7), probably a vast, but invisible, canopy of water vapor surrounding the earth as part of its upper atmosphere. Water vapor, as distinct from liquid droplets of water such as in the clouds, is invisible, but can produce important effects. Although it cannot make a rainbow (for this, liquid droplets are required) it produces a strong greenhouse effect, which should assure the earth a worldwide pleasantly warm climate, and would prevent air mass movements which would generate rainfall, especially storm rainfall.

Furthermore, it would effectively filter out the harmful rays from space which are known to have deleterious effects on health and longevity. The precipitation of this vapor canopy at the flood could have been a key factor in the rapid decrease of longevity after the flood. The devastating erosion by the flood of the primeval topsoil with its abundance of necessary nutrients may well have been another factor causing the post-flood decline in longevity, as well as God's allowing the eating of meat (by both men and now-carnivorous animals) after the flood.

Similarly, in the millennium, life spans will be long again, appetites will be herbivorous again, rains will be gentle again, storms will be absent again, and the whole world will be habitable again. "The wilderness and the solitary place will be glad for them; and the desert shall rejoice, and blossom as the rose ... for in the wilderness shall waters break out, and streams in the desert" (Isaiah 35:1,6).

Likewise, the topography will become pleasant and gentle again. The present high mountain ranges of the world were uplifted in the closing stages of the flood year, through great volcanic and tectonic activity in the earth's crust. Similarly, the present great and wide oceans of the world were opened up after the flood to allow the flood waters to return from off the earth (note Psalm 104:5-9).

For the millennial period, "every valley shall be exalted, and every mountain and hill shall be made low: and the crooked shall be made straight, and the rough places plain" (Isaiah 40:4). Apparently, the topography of the earth's surface in the millennium will be quite similar to that in the world before the flood.

Although there was no rain before the flood, there were rivers, apparently fed through artesian springs (note Genesis 2:10) from the "great deep," composed of subterranean pressurized reservoirs that broke up at the time of the flood (Genesis 7:11). This system may also be restored in the millennium (Zechariah 14:8; Ezekiel 47:1-9; etc.).

The idyllic climate and topography of the primeval world were drastically changed by the flood. The vapor condensed and fell to earth, the fountains of the great deep were cleaved open, and the great waters from both devastated the earth. "The world that then was, being overflowed (literally 'cataclysmically overwhelmed') with water, perished" (II Peter 3:6). Later, great mountains were elevated and basins opened up to receive all the drainage waters from the inundated surface. The pre-flood mountains and soils were eroded away, then later deposited in great sedimentary basins. The earth's surface—its hydrology, climatology, geology and most everything else—was vastly changed.

It would seem, therefore, that if millennial conditions are going to be like those before the flood, then somehow the effects of the flood have to be essentially reversed. In particular, the waters above the firmament must be restored. This is at least implied in Psalm 148, the central psalm of the five "hallelujah psalms" at the close of the Book of Psalms.

> *Praise Him, ye heavens of heavens, and ye waters that be above the heavens .... for He commanded, and they were created. He hath also stablished them for ever and ever (Psalm 148:4-6).*

Now, if the "waters above the heavens" are to be established there forever, they must somehow be restored up there, for they were precipitated at the time of the flood, and are not there now.

Similarly, the present mountains must be cut down and all the earth's topography made gentle again. All of this would seem to be impossible, except for God, who created it all to begin with. Surprisingly, many of the physical phenomena described as taking place during the tribulation period could produce these very results.

Shaking Terribly the Earth

The seven-year period prophesied in the seventieth week of Daniel 9 is, as we have seen, the time of the rise and rule of the Antichrist, with the terrible persecutions which he will unleash on all who refuse to worship him. It will involve the "time of Jacob's trouble," and great suffering by the Jews under the iron hand of the Beast.

All who reject the mark of the Beast, Jew or Gentile, will be put to death if they are caught.

But all this is only a secondary aspect of the tribulation.

For yourselves know perfectly that the day of the Lord so cometh as a thief in the night. For when they shall say, Peace and safety: then sudden destruction cometh upon them, as travail upon a woman with child; and they shall not escape (I Thessalonians 5:2-3).

The onset of the seventieth week will also begin the great day of the Lord. God has allowed men and women at least six thousand years of probation, and these have all been years of human rebellion, growing "worse and worse" (II Timothy 3:13), until finally, man's day is done and the day of the Lord begins.

The great day of the Lord is near, ... That day is a day of wrath, a day of trouble and distress, a day of wasteness and desolation, a day of darkness and gloominess, a day of clouds and thick darkness... And I will bring distress upon men, that they should walk like blind men, because they have sinned against the Lord: ... Neither their silver nor their gold shall be able to deliver them in the day of the Lord's wrath (Zephaniah 1:15,17,18).

Alas for the day! for the day of the Lord is at hand, and as a destruction from the Almighty shall it come (Joel 1:15).

For the day of the Lord of hosts shall be upon every one that is proud and lofty, ... and the haughtiness of men shall be made low: and the Lord alone shall be exalted in that day. And the idols He shall utterly abolish. And they shall go into the holes of the rocks, and into the caves of the earth, for fear of the Lord, and for the glory of His majesty, when He ariseth to shake terribly the earth (Isaiah 2:12, 17–19).

There are numerous similar references in Scripture to the coming day of the Lord. In many cases, the predictions have both near and far fulfillments in accord with the principle of double reference so frequently encountered in Scripture, with the precursive fulfillment a sort of mini-model of the ultimate. These past judgments of God have often been severe, but the worldwide judgment yet to come will finally put down all rebellion, "and the LORD alone shall be exalted in that day" (Isaiah 2:17).

The many prophecies in the Old Testament Scriptures concerning these coming judgments are finally brought together, clarified and completed in the Book of Revelation, which describes in full the events of the tribulation period. As noted before, the judgments of the first 3½ years are given under the symbols of the seven broken seals and the seven trumpets (Revelation 6–9), those of the last 3½ years under the symbol of the seven vials of wrath (Revelation 15:7).

Among other results, these great judgments will so change the earth that they will finally restore, in great measure, conditions in the atmosphere and lithosphere and hydrosphere that had prevailed in the antediluvian world.

As we have seen, God's two witnesses will have their ministry during the first 3½ years, arriving back on earth just before the judgments begin. "Behold, I will send you Elijah the prophet before the coming of the great and dreadful day of the LORD" (Malachi 4:5). Enoch and Elijah will be God's chief human agents on the earth. They will soon begin calling, in the sight of men, for the judgments of God, that will be sent down from heaven. God has said concerning this ministry:

> *And I will give power unto my two witnesses, and they shall prophesy a thousand two hundred and threescore days, clothed in sackcloth ... These have power to shut heaven, that it rain not in the days of their prophecy: and have power over waters to turn them to blood, and to smite*

*the earth with all plagues, as often as they will
(Revelation 11:3,6).*

Thus, there will be no rain anywhere on earth for 3½ years. This, of course, will produce famines on the earth, as indicated under the judgment of the third seal and the third of the "four horsemen of the Apocalypse" (Revelation 6:5–6).

Water will still be evaporated from the oceans, of course, ascending into the sky. In the present order of things, these evaporated waters are then translated by the great winds of the earth inland to the continents. In this future day, however, there will be four angels in the four quarters of the earth "holding the four winds of the earth, that the wind should not blow on the earth, nor on the sea" (Revelation 7:1). The water will not be able to move inland to rain on the earth, so must simply ascend high into the upper atmosphere, thus gradually restoring the "waters above the firmament," as in the pre-flood world.

This further means that water levels will be falling in the rivers and lakes and oceans, even the ground water. Pastures will become brown and barren. Grass fires and forest fires will proliferate. In fact, "the third part of trees was burnt up, and all green grass was burnt up" (Revelation 8:7).

*How do the beasts groan! the herds of cattle are
perplexed, because they have no pasture; ... for
the fire hath devoured the pastures of the wilderness, and the flame hath burned all the trees of
the field. The beasts of the field cry also unto*

thee: for the rivers of waters are dried up, ...
(Joel 1:18-20).

Not only will the creeks and small rivers run dry, but even the great rivers of the world will eventually become dry. At the later time of the "seven vial judgments," we read that "the sixth angel poured out his vial upon the great river Euphrates; and the water thereof was dried up" (Revelation 16:12).

Presumably the Tigris and other great rivers of the earth will dry up too. The capital city Babylon will suffer a serious water shortage, as will other major cities. Shortly before this time, "the fourth angel poured out his vial upon the sun; and power was given unto him to scorch men with fire, And men were scorched with great heat, and blasphemed the name of God, which hath power over these plagues: and they repented not to give Him glory" (Revelation 16:8-9).

This great heat will surely also melt the great ice caps of the world, in Greenland and Antarctica, for they also must be removed to prepare the lands of the earth for millennial habitation. For a short time, the ocean levels will rise as they receive these meltwaters, probably inundating and destroying many of the world's coastal cities.

And the LORD God of hosts is he that toucheth
the land, and it shall melt, and all that dwell
therein shall mourn: and it shall rise up wholly
like a flood; and shall be drowned, as by the
flood of Egypt. It is He ... that calleth for the
waters of the sea, and poureth them out upon

the face of the earth: The LORD is His name
(Amos 9:5-6).

Mighty Babylon itself, after its fiery destruction, will eventually be covered with these waters. "The sea is come up upon Babylon: she is covered with the multitude of the waves thereof" (Jeremiah 51:42).

There will be another great phenomenon taking place during the seven years, as earthquakes and sky-darkening volcanism increase. With the opening of the sixth seal, early in the tribulation period, these will become extremely severe.

Lo, there was a great earthquake; and the sun
became black as sackcloth of hair, and the moon
became as blood; ... and every mountain and
island were moved out of their places (Revelation
6:12,14).

Evidently the crust of the earth will begin to slide over its mantle. To people on the earth it will seem as though "the heavens departed as a scroll when it is rolled together" (verse 14).

Simultaneously, the long-feared asteroid bombardment of the earth will occur, for it says "the stars of heaven fell upon the earth, even as a fig tree casteth her untimely figs, when she is shaken of a mighty wind:" (Revelation 6:13). Men will recognize that these are God's judgments, as His two witnesses will have been proclaiming, and people will cry out that "the great Day of His wrath is come; and who shall be able to stand" (Revelation 6:17).

And I will shew wonders in the heavens and in the earth, blood, and fire, and pillars of smoke. The sun shall be turned into darkness, and the moon into blood, before the great and the terrible day of the LORD come .... The LORD also shall roar out of Zion, and utter His voice from Jerusalem: and the heavens and the earth shall shake: but the LORD will be the hope of His people, and the strength of the children of Israel: (Joel 2:30–31; 3:16).

The coastal lands will become even more unstable than they are now, and will begin sloughing off into the oceans.

The earth is utterly broken down, the earth is clean dissolved, the earth is moved exceedingly. The earth shall reel to and fro like a drunkard: (Isaiah 24:19).

As these violent geophysical phenomena continue at intervals through the tribulation period, finally will come the greatest earthquake of all.

And the seventh angel poured out his vial into the air; ... and there was a great earthquake, such as was not since men were upon the earth, so mighty an earthquake, and so great.... And every island fled away, and the mountains were not found (Revelation 16:18,20).

For thus saith the LORD of hosts: ... I will shake the heavens, and the earth, and the sea and the

dry land; and I will shake all nations, and the
desire of nations shall come (Haggai 2:6,7).

This unprecedented shaking will break down all land mountains and islands (i.e., ocean floor mountains) and transport them down into the depths of the sea, thus significantly filling up the deep ocean basins. At the same time, it seems likely that the global shifting of earth's crust will generate large crustal voids into which many waters will descend. The felling mountains will trap them there, once again producing great subterranean pressurized reservoirs of water, such as existed in the "great deep" before the flood.

On the continental surfaces, the prophecy of Isaiah will thus be fulfilled, when he said: "Every valley shall be exalted, and every mountain and hill shall be made low: and the crooked shall be made straight, and the rough places plain" (Isaiah 40:4). The great mountains will become gentle hills, the ice-covered polar lands will become fertile plains, the deep and wide oceans will become shallow, narrow seas, the deserts will have springs breaking out from restored fountains of the great deep, and the water vapor blanket will have been restored in the sky. By the end of the seven years of God's judgments on the earth, most or all of the conditions which God had created for the beautiful primeval world will have been restored and the world will have been prepared for its grand kingdom age and the 1000-year reign of Christ here on the earth.

These are the main physical changes that will take place, but there are others, too. The waters of the earth will be polluted with blood, for example, as well as gases from a comet falling into the sea (Revelation 8:7–11; 16:3–4), and all sea creatures will die (verse 3). Apparently only freshwater animals and perhaps ocean mammals will survive.

During this same period, the world ruler called the Beast will have been preparing, under the guidance of the old Dragon, for their great confrontation at Armageddon with the returning Christ. These political movements, however, are beyond our purposes of discussion here (please see my book *The Revelation Record* for a detailed exposition of these events).

The Millennial World Order

The dream of the New-Agers and other utopian planners to develop a new world order, centered in a global government, with an international economic order, a worldwide humanistic culture, and a single religion based on evolutionary pantheism and polytheism will finally have been achieved by the Antichrist, who is the Beast, the Man of Sin and the Son of Perdition. The world will not only worship him, but also the powerful demonic spirit energizing him, who is none other than Satan, that old Serpent, the great Dragon, the Devil. Men on earth will finally recognize that God exists in the heavens, but will knowingly cast their lot with Satan (i.e., the Lucifer of so many secret societies and New-age cults) in his rebellion against God, convinced that in the cosmic evolutionary struggle, Satan and his hosts will prove to be the fittest who survive.

But this new world order will very soon be found unfit to survive! Men may reject God's Word, but they cannot refute it. "For what if some did not believe? shall their unbelief make the faith of God without effect? God forbid. Yea, let God be true but every man a liar" (Romans 3:3,4). The Holy Scriptures clearly tell us "those things which must shortly come to pass" (Revelation 1:1).

By the end of the tribulation period, the great cities of the world will mostly be in shambles under the blows of the last great earthquake (Revelation 16:19), and finally even Babylon will be burned to rubble, then inundated by great sea waves. But Jerusalem will survive! In fact, the earthquake there will merely open a great fountain for its inhabitants, as Christ comes to set His throne there.

And His feet shall stand in that day upon the Mount of Olives, ... and the Mount of Olives shall cleave in the midst thereof toward the east and toward the west, and there shall be a very great valley; and half of the mountain shall remove toward the north, and half of it toward the south.... And it shall be in that day, that living waters shall go out from Jerusalem: half of them toward the former sea, and half of them toward the hinder sea: in summer and winter shall it be. And, the LORD shall be king over all the earth: in that day shall there be one LORD, and His name one.... And men shall dwell in it, and there shall be no more utter destruction: but Jerusalem shall be safely inhabited (Zechariah 14:4,8,9,11).

All the armies of the world will have converged on the land of Israel, under the instruction of Satan, through the Beast and his false Prophet, using the multitude of demonic spirits who do their bidding, as they "gather them to the battle of that great day of God Almighty ... into a place called in the Hebrew tongue Armageddon" (Revelation 16:14,16). Armageddon, of course, is the great valley about 40 miles north of Jerusalem.

There they will, indeed, plan to battle the returning Christ and His saints, but the Lord will slay them all simply by His Word, for "out of His mouth goeth a sharp sword, that with it He should smite the nations" (Revelation 19:15). "He shall smite the earth with the word of His mouth, and with the breath of His lips shall He slay the wicked" (Isaiah 11:4). "And then shall that Wicked (one) be revealed, whom the Lord shall consume with the spirit of His mouth, and shall destroy with the brightness of His coming" (II Thessalonians 2:8).

So the legendary battle of Armageddon, the name of which seems to be invoked whenever war breaks out, will not be a battle at all! The great Creator, the Lord Jesus Christ, will merely speak, and the victory is done. His Word had called the cosmos into being, and His Word is sufficient to slay all His enemies.

And the Beast was taken, and with him the False Prophet ..., These both were cast alive into (the) lake of fire burning with brimstone.... And he laid hold on the Dragon, that old Serpent, which is the Devil, and Satan, and bound him a thousand years, and cast him into the bottomless pit, and shut him up, and set a seal upon him, that he should deceive the nations no more, till the thousand years should be fulfilled (Revelation 19:20; 20:2,3).

The spirits of the slain, like all those who die without Christ, will descend into the great pit of Hades in the heart of the earth, while their bodies will be consumed by great flocks of scavenger birds (Revelation 19:17,18,21). Satan also will be cast into this "bottomless pit" (Greek *Abussos*, 'without bottom') at the center of the earth, where every boundary must be a great ceiling structure.

Those among the nations who are still living, but had received the mark of the Beast, will be cast alive into "everlasting fire, prepared for the devil and his angels" (Revelation 19:9–11; Matthew 25:41); to which the Beast and his False Prophet have preceded them.

There will, however, still be some people living who have escaped the Beast and his mark. This will especially be true of the "woman in the wilderness," the believing Israelites who have been supernaturally protected for the last 3½ years in the mountains and deserts of Jordan. It will probably also be true of some in every nation, those who have become true believers in Christ, and even possibly others who are willing to believe God when they hear the truth and who have shown a spirit of Christian compassion during the times of famine and persecution (Matthew 25:34-40). To these, Christ will say: "Come, ye blessed of my Father, inherit the kingdom prepared for you from the foundation of the world" (Matthew 25:34). "Every one that is left of all the nations which came against Jerusalem shall even go up from year to year to worship the King, The LORD of hosts, and to keep the feast of tabernacles" (Zechariah 14:16).

The population of believers, still living in the flesh and allowed thus to participate in the millennial kingdom, will initially be small, for "therefore hath the curse devoured the earth, and they that dwell therein are desolate: therefore the inhabitants of the earth are burned, and few men left" (Isaiah 24:6).

But with these few, the Lord Jesus Christ will establish his own "new world order," a great kingdom of peace and righteousness on earth that will last a thousand years. His capital will be at Jerusalem, "for out of Zion shall go forth the law and the word of the LORD from Jerusalem" (Isaiah 2:3).

Mankind will finally be able to enjoy a new world order in which war and crime are banished—not by U.N. resolutions or government police forces, but by Christ Himself, who will "rule them with a rod of iron" (Revelation 19:15). All those entering the kingdom, both Jews and Gentiles, will have been "born again" through personal faith in Christ as Savior and Lord, and will be freed from the corrupting influences of false teachings in the schools and harmful temptations and peer pressures in society. The environment will again be healthy and harmonious, conducive to longevity and great productivity.

True education, "thinking God's thoughts after him," will be available to all. Scientific research and discovery will thrive to a far greater degree than ever before in history, for the scientists and technologists will all seek to honor God in their studies and inventions. All the benefits of modern civilization, with innumerable new fruits of scientific research, will be available to all, without the damaging effects on mind and body that accompany them today. The great "dominion mandate" given in Eden (Genesis 1:26–28), God's first great commission to mankind, will finally be carried out in the way God had intended. Populations will rapidly multiply, as new generations are born and all generations continue to work together for God's glory and the benefit of mankind.

It is interesting to note that animal sacrifice will be restored as part of the temple worship in Jerusalem. (See the extensive specifications for this in Ezekiel, Chapters 42–46). Furthermore, there will apparently be an annual participation of all the nations in at least some aspects of the Jewish worship (e.g., Zechariah 14:16–19).

The specific reasons for the restoration of the sacrifices are not given, but they probably are intended to remind people of the one great Sacrifice made by Christ long ago. He will be present in the world in all His glory, and it may become difficult for people to remember that His body of humiliation once had to be made a sacrificial offering for their sins. This will especially be true of the new generations that will be born, since they never will have known a world of sin and suffering. The death of innocent animals on an altar may serve to teach them something of the great sacrifice made by the King on their behalf. It also may be used to lead them to acceptance of Him as their personal Savior from sin.

It will be all but impossible for men in the millennial age to deny His deity, for they can see Him in His glory reigning over the earth, but it may be much more difficult to believe in His suffering, dying humanity—especially as dying for their own sins. They will still be in the natural flesh, however, still subject to sin, especially to pride, the sin of the devil. The devil will be confined in Hades during this time, but men and women still will have inherited sin-natures. Men and women must be saved during the millennium in the same way as in all other ages, through repentance and faith in Christ as their personal Savior from sin. The animal sacrifices may well help them to see and understand this.

Another unusual phenomenon will occur in the temple. "Behold, waters issued out from under the threshold of the house eastward" (Ezekiel 47:1). These are apparently the same waters referred to in Zechariah 14:8,9, soon becoming two great rivers, one flowing to the Mediterranean, one into the Dead Sea. They are pure waters, actually "healing" the salty waters and supporting an abundance of fish that will presumably migrate from fresh-water lakes and then multiply there. This may suggest that, after the destruction of all sea creatures in the tribulation, followed by the drastic redistribution of the earth's waters, some into the great deep, some into the vapor canopy, all the waters will somehow be healed of their salt content, and all millennial fish populations will live in fresh water, "for they shall be healed; and every thing shall live whither the river cometh" (Ezekiel 47:9). Perhaps these healing waters, issuing from God's sanctuary in Jerusalem, will, with supernaturally imparted healing qualities, eventually make all of earth's waters pure and fresh again.

As the centuries roll by, however, successive new generations will be born, with the hard-learned lessons of the former age, taught by their parents, gradually retreating further and further from their minds and hearts. They are still in the flesh, still with inherited sin-natures, still subject to fleshly temptations. Although outwardly forced to conform to godly standards of righteousness, many will become inwardly rebellious, wanting somehow to shake off their restraints.

This is the reason why Satan must be released once more. "And when the thousand years are expired, Satan shall be loosed out of his prison, And shall go out to deceive the nations which are in the four quarters of the earth, Gog and Magog, to gather them together to battle: the number of whom is as the sand of the sea." (Revelation 20:7,8).

What an indictment of the sinful human heart! After 1000 years in a perfect environment, with great prosperity and peace for all, there will still remain an innumerable multitude of people who are ready to rebel once more against the Lord and His Christ.

CHAPTER 7

Life in the Holy City

The Last Judgment and the Lake of Fire

The great rebellion against God after a thousand years of an all-but-perfect world will evidently exhaust the patience of even our long-suffering God of all grace. The time will finally have come to "make an end of sins, and to make reconciliation for iniquity, and to bring in everlasting righteousness" (Daniel 9:24). When Satan and his innumerable host come up to surround the holy city, John says, "fire came down from God out of heaven and devoured them" (Revelation 20:9). Futhermore it will devour the whole earth, for this will apparently be the time when the prophecy of Peter is fulfilled.

> But the day of the Lord will come as a thief in the night [that is, it begins unexpectedly, ushering in the tribulation and millennial periods, all of which are included in that great 'day']; in the which the heavens shall pass away with a great

> *noise, and the elements will melt with fervent*
> *heat, the earth also and the works that are*
> *therein shall be burned up (II Peter 3:10).*

All the age-long effects of sin that have impregnated the very rocks of the earth's crust (e.g., the great beds of fossils, which were buried by the flood, but which have been distorted by unbelievers into a supposed record of the evolutionary ages of geology) must be burned out of it, and the curse of decay must be purged from the very elements.

Satan also must finally be destroyed. "And the Devil that deceived them was cast into the lake of fire and brimstone, where the Beast and the False Prophet are, and shall be tormented day and night for ever and ever" (Revelation 20:10). The earth and its atmospheric heaven will have "fled away" when God appears on His "great white throne" of judgment (verse 11), yet the Beast and the False Prophet still remain in the lake of fire, where Satan will now join them. This fact makes it clear that the lake of fire is neither on this present earth nor on the new earth which God will create. Nevertheless, it is a real place in this universe, and it will be there forever.

It will be far away from the earth, for those who spend eternity there must "be punished with everlasting destruction from the presence of the Lord and from the glory of His power" (II Thessalonians 1:9). In this verse, the word "destruction" does not mean "annihilation," but rather "disintegration" or "ruin," with no further possibility of restoration. Since the "glory of the Lord" will be centered in the New Jerusalem, on the new earth, the lake of fire must be in some distant corner of the universe, far away from the presence of God. Possibly it will be a star (a star is, after all, a great lake of fire) where all those who have rejected their Creator/Redeemer, will be confined throughout eternity—the Devil and his angels (Matthew 25:41),—as well as unsaved men and women.

First, however, there will be a great judgment day, when "the dead, small and great, stand before God." All the lost souls of the ages will be delivered up out of Hades, where they have been confined in the heart of the earth since the death of their bodies, "the first death." To appear before God's judgment throne, their dead bodies must be miraculously revived, and they will stand before God in their fleshly bodies. "Many of them that sleep in the dust of the earth shall awake, some to everlasting life, and some to shame and everlasting contempt" (Daniel 12:2). Jesus said: "The hour is coming, in the which all that are in the graves shall hear His voice, and shall come forth; they that have done good, unto the resurrection of life; and they that have done evil, unto the resurrection of damnation" (John 5:29).

The very concept of resurrection implies the miraculous power of the Creator. It is significant that it is only the three creationist religions (Islam, Judaism, Christianity) that believe in the doctrine of bodily resurrection. All other religions are based on evolutionary pantheism and, although they all believe in some form of immortality (evolution to a spirit plane, reincarnation, etc.), they concede that resurrection of the body—especially after its disintegration and return to dust—is impossible. No one but the Creator of physical, biological life can possibly re-create physical, biological life.

But He can, and He will!

What an amazing gathering this will be, with billions of unsaved men and women, young and old, standing before the eternal Judge on His great white throne, awaiting sentence.

> *And I saw the dead, small and great, stand before God; and the books were opened: ... and the dead were judged out of those things which were written in the books, according to their works (Revelation 20:12).*

But not one can measure up to God's standards of perfect righteousness, "for all have sinned, and come short of the glory of God" (Romans 3:23).

The dead will be judged according to their works, but no one is saved by works, for "by the works of the law shall no flesh be justified" (Galations 2:16). "And whosoever was not found written in the Book of Life was cast into the lake of fire" (Revelation 20:15). That book is "the book of life of the Lamb slain from the foundation of the world" (Revelation 13:8), and clearly contains only the names of those who are trusting for forgiveness and cleansing in the Lamb of God as their Substitute and Savior. These believing disciples, however, will already have been resurrected a thousand years earlier (Revelation 20:4,5) in the "first resurrection." Only the dead will be judged at the great white throne, and all of these will be cast into the great fire, which is "the second death" (Revelation 20:14).

They will be judged according to their works, however, and will therefore suffer in various measures according to their degree of guilt in relation to the amount of light they had received and rejected. Exactly how this will be achieved in a fiery lake, will have to be left to God. If, as many argue, these fires are only symbolic fires, then the reality which they symbolize must be at least as fearsome—so fearsome that the only appropriate symbol is the most terrible penalty we can imagine.

The concept of eternal suffering in the fires of hell is, of course, very offensive to those who reject God and His provision of salvation—that is, to those who are going there! Their charge of unfairness and cruelty, however, must be viewed in the light of the infinitude of their crime. "He that believeth not is condemned already, because he hath not believed in the name of the only begotten Son of God" (John 3:18).

They have rebelled against the one who created them, and then compounded their guilt by spurning His infinite love for them when He suffered the agonies of hell on the cross for them! They have either refused or ignored His offer of forgiveness and eternal life, which He would have given to them as a free gift if they would only have accepted it by faith. A million so-called "good works" could never obliterate the infinitely evil work of rejecting the infinite love of their Creator and Redeemer. And it is equally bad—perhaps worse—to ignore Him as it is to openly reject Him. Even those who never hear the explicit message of the Gospel are "without excuse" (Romans 1:20, because they have rejected or ignored even the evidence of the Creator/-Redeemer in nature and in their consciences, rejecting even the dim light they have. "Men loved darkness rather than light, because their deeds were evil" (John 3:19).

In any case, whether or not we fully understand it, all who reject or ignore God's saving work in Christ will spend eternity in the lake of fire, after they face Him at the last judgment. "For the Father ... hath committed all judgment to the Son" (John 5:22), and He has made this emphatically clear. Jesus, the Son of God, had more to say about hell than any other Biblical writer. For example: "Then shall He say unto them on the left hand, Depart from me, ye cursed, into everlasting fire" (Matthew 25:41). Jesus Christ is our Creator, our Redeemer and our sooncoming Judge. Men and women need to hear Him when He speaks, whether they like what He says or not!

The First Resurrection

In describing the awesome events at the last judgment, the Apostle John made no mention of the saints, the multitudes who had believed in Christ and whose names were written in the Lamb's Book of Life. Evidently they were not even present at the scene, except possibly as distant on-lookers. Jesus had taught, when He was on the earth at His first coming, that there would be two resurrections—"the resurrection of life" and "the resurrection of damnation" (John 5:29). But it was not revealed at that time that there would be a thousand years between the two. The first would be completed at the end of the tribulation period, the second at the end of the millennial period.

> *But the rest of the dead lived not again until the thousand years were finished. This is the first resurrection. Blessed and holy is he that hath part in the first resurrection: on such the second death hath no power, but they shall be priests of God and of Christ, and shall reign with him a thousand years (Revelation 20:5,6).*

This passage makes it clear that there will not be a "general resurrection" of both saved and unsaved, followed by a "general judgment" of both groups at the same time. The first resurrection relates only to the saved, the second—a thousand years later—only to the lost, who are then condemned to the lake of fire.

As a matter of fact, even the first resurrection will involve more than one stage. "For as in Adam all die, even so in Christ shall all be made alive. But every man in his own order: Christ the firstfruits; afterward they that are Christ's at His coming" (I Corinthians 15:22-23). The phrase "they that are Christ's" seems to refer specifically to those who have been called out to believe on Him in this age of the Christian church, as distinct from those who looked forward to His coming back in the age of Israel's theocracy. His "Old

Testament saints" were evidently resurrected shortly after Christ's own resurrection. At that time, according to Matthew:

> *The graves were opened; and many bodies of the saints which slept arose, And came out of the graves after His resurrection, and went into the holy city, and appeared unto many (Matthew 27:52–53).*

The graves were opened by the earthquake at the time of Christ's *death*, but the bodies of these saints arose only after His *resurrection*, for He must be the "firstfruits."

During the three days between Christ's death and His resurrection, He went in His spirit into the heart of the earth to proclaim His victory to the rebellious "spirits in prison" (I Peter 3:18), the demonic host confined there ever since they "kept not their first estate, but left their own habitation," seeking to destroy God's plans for the human race "in the days of Noah" (Jude 6; I Peter 3:19; Genesis 6:1,4). After He had "descended first into the lower parts of the earth" (Ephesians 4:9), completing His mission there "to proclaim liberty to the captives, and the opening of the prison to them that are bound" (Isaiah 61:1), He then returned to His sleeping body in Joseph's tomb, and arose from the dead. Furthermore, "when He ascended up on high, He led captivity captive" (Ephesians 4:8). The spirits of the righteous (i.e., believing) saints which were awaiting Him in Hades were then reunited with their own sleeping bodies in the graves, from which they also arose, and appeared unto many in Jerusalem. All the Old Testament saints, from Abraham to John the Baptist—all who died in faith prior to Christ's death—were raised with Him, then after a brief interval, also with Him "ascended up far above all heavens" (Ephesians 4:10) to the throne of God. This brief interval of their appearance in Jerusalem—no doubt as a testimony of the reality of the resurrection of Christ that would soon be preached in great power by those who had seen Him after His resurrection—was probably the same as that mentioned to Mary Magdalene, who was the first to see Christ. "Touch me not;" He said; "for I am not yet ascended to my Father: but go to my brethren, and say unto them, I ascend unto my Father, and your Father: and to my God, and your God" (John 20:17). This initial ascension, taking the rescued and resurrected saints with Him, was for only a brief period. He then returned to the earth, being seen by the disciples in His resurrected body many times during a forty-day period (Acts 1:1-3).

Then began the church age, and the preaching of the gospel of Christ. When He ascended again into heaven, after forty days with His disciples, He repeated His promise to come again. Just before His crucifixion, He had said: "I go to prepare a place for you. And ... I will come again, and receive you unto myself:" (John 14:2-3). Following His ascension, He said to them, through His heaven-sent messengers: "This same Jesus, which is taken up from you into heaven, shall so come in like manner as ye have seen Him go into heaven" (Acts 1:11).

For some time after that, it appears that the disciples were looking for His return during their own lifetime, even though He had commanded them to carry His message "to the uttermost parts of the earth" (Acts 1:8). But as believers began to die, their survivors began to raise the question about their own promised resurrection. Thus Paul promised them that, as Christ (followed by the saints who had died before Christ) had been the firstfruits of the resurrection promise, all others would follow at Christ's return.

Even before Paul had written this assurance to the Corinthians, he had written these wonderful words to the Thessalonians:

> *If we believe that Jesus died and rose again, even so them also which sleep in Jesus will God bring with him. For this we say unto you by the word of the Lord, that we which are alive and remain unto the coming of the Lord shall not prevent [or 'precede'] them which are asleep. For the Lord Himself shall descend from heaven with a shout, with the voice of the archangel, and with the trump of God: And the dead in Christ shall rise first: Then we which are alive and remain shall be caught up together with them in the clouds, to meet the Lord in the air: and so shall we ever be with the Lord (I Thessalonians 4:14–17).*

Thus, not only will the dead in Christ be raised, but so will those who are still living when he returns. Both will be given glorified bodies like that of Christ Himself.

> *We shall not all sleep, but we shall all be changed. In a moment, in the twinkling of an eye, at the last trump: ... For this corruptible must put on incorruption, and this mortal must put on immortality (I Corinthians 15:51–53).*

> *(The Lord Jesus Christ) shall change our vile body, that it may be fashioned like unto His glorious body, according to the working whereby He is able even to subdue all things unto Himself (Philippians 3:21).*

> *It doth not yet appear, what we shall be: but we know that, when He shall appear, we shall be like Him; for we shall see Him as He is (I John 3:2).*

The resurrection day will indeed be a fantastic day, when we all meet the Lord Jesus, along with all others who are "in Christ," in a wonderful meeting in the air.

The Imminence of His Coming

When Paul wrote to the church at Thessalonica, it was relatively early in His ministry, and he was evidently even then looking for the Lord's return. "We which are alive and remain shall be caught up together with them in the clouds to meet the Lord in the air," he wrote (I Thessalonians 4:17).

Many years later, as he wrote his last epistle, he was in a Roman dungeon awaiting the executioner. There he wrote: "The time of my departure is at hand ... Henceforth there is laid up for me a crown of righteousness, which the Lord, the righteous judge, shall give me at that day: and not to me only, but unto all them also that love His appearing" (II Timothy 4:6,8).

Paul didn't live to see the return of Christ, but he "loved His appearing," and so should we, for "every man that hath this hope in him purifieth himself, even as He is pure" (I John 3:3). James also could hold out this hope to those who were suffering for Christ in his day. "Be ye also patient, stablish your hearts: for the coming of the Lord draweth nigh" (James 5:8). John began the final book of the Bible with God's promise "to shew unto his servants things which must shortly come to pass," and concluded it with His promise: "Surely I come quickly" (Revelation 1:1; 22:20). "Looking for that blessed hope, and the glorious appearing of the great God and our Savior Jesus Christ" has in every generation been for Christians a major incentive to "live soberly, righteously and godly, in this present world" (Titus 2:12,13).

On the other hand, the Lord Jesus severely warned His servants not to say in their hearts: "My lord delayeth His coming" (Luke 12:45), lest they get their hearts set on this present evil world instead of their Lord. He stressed the any-moment imminence of His coming many times. For example, every believer should carefully consider the following admonitions of the Lord Jesus:

> *But of that day and hour knoweth no man, no, not the angels of heaven, but my Father only (Matthew 24:36).*
>
> *Watch therefore: for ye know not what hour your Lord doth come (Matthew 24:42).*
>
> *Therefore be ye also ready: for in such an hour as ye think not, the Son of man cometh (Matthew 24:44).*
>
> *Watch therefore, for ye know neither the day nor the hour wherein the Son of man cometh (Matthew 25:13).*
>
> *But of that day and that hour knoweth no man, no, not the angels which are in heaven, neither the Son, but the Father. Take ye heed, watch and pray: for ye know not when the time is (Mark 13:32–33).*
>
> *Watch ye therefore: for ye know not when the master of the house cometh, at even, or at midnight, or at the cockcrowing, or in the morning: Lest coming suddenly He find you sleeping. And what I say unto you I say unto all, Watch (Mark 13:35–37).*
>
> *Blessed are those servants, whom the Lord when He cometh shall find watching: ... And if He shall come in the second watch, or come in the*

third watch, and find them so, blessed are those servants ... Be ye therefore ready also: for the Son of man cometh at an hour when ye think not (Luke 12:37,38,40).

It is obviously the Lord's will—indeed His command—for us to be constantly watchful, aware of the possibility that He might return at any time. "And now, little children, abide in Him; that, when He shall appear, we may have confidence, and not be ashamed before Him at His coming" (I John 2:28).

This doctrine of constant readiness and alertness has been a comforting and purifying and activating truth for every generation of Christians. It is obvious that no specific prophesied events were required to take place before His coming—such as the revealing of the Antichrist, the seven-year treaty with the Jews, the invasion of Israel by Gog and Magog, the battle of Armageddon, or anything else. If it were not so, there would be no need to be watching for Christ; we would need first to watch for some event in the world to occur before He could return. The various signs of the last days, such as the increase of science and travel, the increase of ungodliness and apostasy, the increased economic strife in the world, the rise of world wars, and other such signs, all indicate that His coming is near, yet paradoxically His return has never been conditioned on the fulfillment of these or any other prophesied signs.

This may seem paradoxical, or even contradictory, but the problem vanishes when we recognize that His second coming—just like His first coming—will include a whole series of events, not simply an instantaneous end-of-the-world judgment. The very first necessary event in that series—that for which all Christians have been exhorted to watch—is His descent from heaven into the earth's atmosphere, with both dead and living believers being resurrected and glorified, then caught up (or "raptured") to meet Him in the air. The various prophesied signs of His coming may or may not (but need not) take place before this. If they do begin to take place before this, then we know His return is that much nearer, for the signs relate to the total aspect of His coming; especially the climactic event when He will come to the earth itself and put down all rebellion at Armageddon.

> *And then shall appear the sign of the Son of man in heaven: and then shall all the tribes of the earth mourn, and they shall see the Son of man coming in the clouds of heaven with power and great glory. (Matthew 24:30).*

> *The Lord Jesus shall be revealed from heaven with His mighty angels, In flaming fire taking vengeance on them that know not God, and that obey not the gospel of our Lord Jesus Christ (II Thessalonians 1:7,8).*

At least some of the events associated with Christ's coming must, therefore, take place only after the first necessary event, the resurrection and rapture of His followers of this age, both dead and living. In particular, the seven-year treaty of the Antichrist with Israel must be signed after the rapture, thus revealing specifically the identity of the Antichrist. The return of Israel in unbelief to their land, followed by Gog's invasion and defeat, also must take place before the seven-year treaty is signed. However, these may or may not take place before the rapture.

The reason God will call for the resurrection and rapture to take place before the seven-year period of the treaty is that these will be the years of God's wrath on an unbelieving world that is in specific and climactic rebellion against its Creator and Redeemer Jesus Christ. It is "the great and the terrible day of the Lord" (Joel 2:31), the "great day of ... the wrath of the Lamb" (Revelation 6:17,16).

Believers of the church age, however, are not the objects of His wrath (there may be tares among the wheat, of course, but we are speaking here only of those who are truly born-again believers). As Paul wrote, in his first epistle:

For yourselves know perfectly that the day of the Lord so cometh as a thief in the night. For when they shall say, Peace and safety; then sudden destruction cometh upon them, as travail upon a woman with child; and they shall not escape. But ye, brethren, are not in darkness, that that day should overtake you as a thief ... For God hath not appointed us to wrath, but to obtain salvation by our Lord Jesus Christ, Who died for us, that, whether we wake or sleep [that is, whether we are still living or already in our graves when He comes], we should live together with Him (I Thessalonians 5:2-4, 9-10).

This assurance, of course, refers back to the previous verses where Paul had written of the coming resurrection and rapture to meet Christ in the air, and to live together with Him (I Thessalonians 4:15-17). This promise specifically assured these believers that they were not to experience the divine wrath of the tribulation period that is coming on unbelievers. That period is to be specifically a time of plagues and judgment and destruction on a world in conflict with God, not a time of chastisement on God's people.

It is true that all believers of all the centuries (not just the last days) "must through much tribulation enter into the kingdom of God" (Acts 14:22) and that "all that will live godly in Christ Jesus shall suffer persecution" (II Timothy 3:12), but such persecutions are imposed on believers by the world, not by the Lord. The sufferings of the seven-year tribulation period, on the other hand, will be imposed by the Creator primarily on that rebelling world.

There will be many people saved during the tribulation period, of course, and they will suffer persecution by the ungodly, just as believers have in all generations. But the wrath of God will be directed against the Beast, and his kingdom, not against those who become believers in that time. To the question as to why believers of this present age should not have to participate in the coming tribulation period, the reply would be "Why should they, when believers of all previous ages did not have to do so?" Christians in every generation have experienced suffering and persecution (some more than others), and the same will be true of the last generation. Those believers who come out of the great tribulation itself (Revelation 7:14) will be in the tribulation only because they neglected to come to Christ before the days of wrath began, while they were still unbelievers. They will be thankful that God gave them this last opportunity, even though it does mean living in the period of tribulation.

To the church at Philadelphia (a real church in Asia Minor in the first century, but also representing all similar churches in every age), Christ promised: "Because thou has kept the Word of my patience, I also will keep thee from the hour of temptation which shall come upon all the world, to try them that dwell upon the earth" (Revelation 3:10).

The pre-tribulation removal of the true church from the earth will mean also, as we have seen, that the Holy Spirit, who indwells all true believers, will remove from the world His restraining influence on evil. As noted earlier, when the Holy Spirit "be taken out of the way, ... than shall that Wicked (One) be revealed" (II Thessalonians 2:7,8), and the evil conquests of the Beast can begin.

Thus, although the resurrection and the accompanying meeting in the air will take place sometime before the seven-year period begins; it seems likely that the Beast will himself become known very soon after the departure of the Holy Spirit and His people. It may even be that the excitement and confusion caused by the sudden disappearance of many people and by the opening of many graves could create the opportunity he needs to come into world prominence as the one who can "explain" these amazing events in a new-age, occultic context that will draw global attention to himself.

In any case, all genuine disciples of Christ will suddenly be gone, along with all their restraining influences on the full development of evil in the world. The various "signs" of His coming will become more intense than ever, and the movement toward a "new world order" of evolutionary humanistic pantheism will accelerate. But this will also be the time, with all other witnesses gone from the earth, that Enoch and Elijah will return to earth to begin the final phase of their great prophetic witness of coming divine judgment.

The Meeting in the Air

So the next great event for which we, as believers in Christ, should be looking is the same as that for which Paul and John and believers in Christ in every generation have been looking—the resurrection of the dead in Christ and the meeting in the air of all His saints with Him. We should stress, of course, that this amazing event will not include all who profess Christ, but only those who possess His indwelling Holy Spirit as a result of their new birth, received on the basis of personal faith in Christ as their redeeming Savior and resurrected Lord. To any who are not yet sure where they stand, Paul would urge: "Examine yourselves, whether ye be in the faith" (II Corinthians 13:5), and Jesus Himself would say: "Watch ye therefore, and pray always, that ye may be accounted worthy to escape all these things that shall come to pass, and to stand before the Son of man" (Luke 21:36).

This will be an indescribably glorious meeting! Our dead loved ones will be caught up first, then we "together with them" will "meet the Lord in the air." It will be a time of grand reunion; my dear wife will see her parents and (we trust) her brothers and sister again, I will see my parents and two younger brothers again, and we both will especially delight in being reunited with our own youngest son, who went to be with Christ very recently, cut off by a vicious cancer in the prime of life. Many, many friends from past years will be there, all young and vigorous again, their bodies no longer subject to pain or injury or even aging. And we ourselves will have new bodies, also young and strong again. So will every other believer, past or present,— all who are "in Christ."

It is probable, too, that all those saints who died before Christ, whose bodies were raised at the time of His own resurrection, will return with Him, so that all the saints of all the ages will assemble there with Christ in the heavens. Our new bodies will be transformed "like unto His glorious body" so that we, like Him after His resurrection, will no longer be constrained by gravity or other natural forces. We shall be able to move through space and to walk through closed doors, as He did. They will still be our own physical bodies, but controlled evidently by spiritual, rather than natural, forces. And, of course, they will no longer be subject to disease, pain, decay and death.

How can all this be? Only because Christ is the Creator, and He can do this "according to the working whereby He is able even to subdue all things unto Himself" (Philippians 3:21). Our present bodies actually "consist in Him" (Colossians 1:17), for "in Him we live, and move, and have our being" (Acts 17:28), and He is "upholding all things by the Word of His power" (Hebrews 1:3), so He can surely accomplish this great miracle also when He "descends from heaven with a shout" (I Thessalonians 4:16).

The multitudes left on earth will probably be mystified and alarmed for a time, but they will soon have other more immediate concerns, with the great plagues being called down on the earth by God's two witnesses. Perhaps their New-Age channelers will speak about the removal of these recalcitrant fundamentalists by UFO's to some other spiritual dimension for re-education, or some such sophistry and people will soon forget, not realizing—at least for a while— the great event taking place high in the air.

These passages in the epistles do not indicate just where in the air this meeting will take place. But there is an intriguing possiblity. Just before His crucifixion, He told His disciples:

> *In my Father's house are many mansions: ... I go to prepare a place for you. And ... I will come again, and receive you unto myself; that where I am, there ye may be also (John 14:2,3).*

That "place" He has gone to prepare is none other than the Holy City, New Jerusalem, for that is where His people will live with Him forever.

And I John saw the holy city, new Jerusalem, coming down from God out of heaven, ... And I heard a great voice out of heaven saying, Behold the tabernacle of God is with men, and He will dwell with them: (Revelation 21:2,3).

When the holy city comes down to the earth at the end of the millennial period, the earth will also be the new earth, not this present world. But the Lord Jesus will also be with His people all through the tribulation and millennial periods. The logical implication is that He will bring the Holy City with Him to the atmospheric environs of the earth. When He comes again to call His people up to meet Him, they will meet Him there, in the place He has prepared for them, suspended high in the air, perhaps even orbiting the earth like a gigantic space platform.

This city is a real place, prepared by the Lord Himself for His people. It exists today, somewhere in this real universe that God created, and it is there where the Lord Jesus, in His real resurrection body of glory, sits on the right hand of the Father, ever living to make intercession for us (Hebrews 7:25).

It is also, presumably, the "paradise" in "the third heaven" to which the Apostle Paul once was "caught up," and where he "heard unspeakable words, which it is not lawful for a man to utter" (II Corinthians 12:2,4). There also, probably, are Enoch and Elijah, still in their supernaturally preserved natural bodies, waiting to complete their ministries on the earth during the coming tribulation period. The Old Testament saints, resurrected and in their glorified eternal bodies, ever since the resurrection of Christ, must also be there.

Finally, the spirits of the "dead in Christ" of this age are there, awaiting the resurrection of their own bodies. We know, at least, that they are "with Christ," for Jesus told the thief on the cross: "Today shalt thou be with me in paradise" (Luke 23:43). Paul said that he had "a desire to depart, and to be with Christ" (Philippians 1:23), because, although for him "to live is Christ, ... to die is gain" (Philippians 1:21).

In some way, the spirits of these departed Christians, although their natural bodies are still in their graves and they have not yet received their glorified bodies, are "clothed" in a celestial body while they rest from their labors and sufferings on earth. "For we know that if our earthly house of this tabernacle were dissolved, we have a building of God, an house not made with hands, eternal in the heavens. ... We are confident, I say, and willing rather to be absent from the body, and to be present with the Lord" (II Corinthians 5:1,8).

All of these are, no doubt, eagerly awaiting the great day of "the coming of our Lord Jesus with all His saints" (I Thessalonians 3:13), when the holy city and its inhabitants will speed swiftly to the earth's atmosphere to meet the resurrected saints of this age. In the meantime, they constitute "so great a cloud of witnesses" in the heavens, no doubt greatly concerned that we who still are living here on earth "run with patience the race that is set before us" (Hebrews 12:1). Although they cannot see us here on earth (unless they have access to some kind of miraculously transmitted recording of events on earth), they may well hear reports concerning our spiritual progress from the angels who observe and guard us.

But one day soon, faith will become sight and all the saints of all ages will be reunited with each other and be with Christ forever. There is going to be a great meeting in the air as the day of the Lord begins on earth.

We also have to face a judgment there before the Lord, not the terrible judgment of the unsaved dead still more than a thousand years in the future, but a judgment for rewards. "For we must all appear before the judgment seat of Christ" (II Corinthians 5:10), where "the fire shall try every man's work of what sort it is. If any man's work abide ... he shall receive a reward. If any man's work shall be burned, he shall suffer loss: but he himself shall be saved; yet so as by fire" (I Corinthians 3:13–15).

This will not be a judgment for salvation, nor to decide a penalty for our sins, for the Judge Himself long ago paid for all our sins on the cross, and has saved us eternally, a gift received entirely by grace through faith. Nor is the reward based on the quantity of our good works. "The fire shall try every man's work of what sort it is." In fact, it will be enough merely to hear Christ say, "Well done, thou good and faithful servant" (Matthew 25:21). For "then shall every man have (his) praise of God" (I Corinthians 4:5).

Is Ours the Last Generation?

Many people have tried to calculate the actual date of the Lord's return, in spite of His specific warning that no one could do this. The command to be watchful every day would be meaningless if the day, or the year, or even the decade, could be calculated ahead of time. All such calculations inevitably must turn out wrong.

But setting dates is not new. The ancient rabbis taught that there would be six thousand years of history—a two-thousand-year age when God was dealing with the whole world, a two-thousand-year age centered in Israel, and a two-thousand-year Messianic age—all followed by a thousand years of universal peace and righteousness. This was believed to correspond to creation week, with each day of creation corresponding to a thousand years of history.

Many commentators, ancient and modern, have interpreted II Peter 3:8 as confirming this tradition. "One day is with the Lord as a thousand years, and a thousand years as one day." This interpretation, if valid, would mean that Christ would return just six thousand years after the creation. In context, however, Peter was not referring to the days of creation, but to the conflict in the last days between uniformitarianism and catastrophism. That is, he was stressing that God can do in one day what uniformitarian reasoning would indicate would require a thousand years. The great flood, by which "the world that then was, being overflowed with water, perished," is the true key for explaining the earth's geologic history, instead of long ages during which "all things continue as they were from the beginning of the creation" (II Peter 3:4,6).

Nevertheless, even though the context does not warrant the six-thousand-year interpretation, it is striking how well it seems to fit. There were, indeed, abut 2000 years from Abraham to Christ and almost 2000 years from Christ to the present, and (if the Ussher chronology is right), 2000 years from Adam to Abraham. In fact, if the Ussher chronology is correct, the creation took place in 4004 B.C., the 6000th year of earth history would be in 1996, and the tribulation would have begun in 1989!

The Ussher date, however, is not part of the inspired text. There have been over 200 published calculations of the date of creation, ranging from 3500 B.C. to 7000 B.C., all supposedly based directly on the Biblical data. This calculation might indicate that His coming is near—just as do many other signs—but it certainly cannot determine the specific date.

There are, as we have noted throughout this book, many signs being fulfilled today that tell us Christ is coming soon. Yet, as we have also seen, the first event of His coming—that is, the resurrection and rapture of the saved of this age— could theoretically have taken place at any time during this age; it did not have to wait for the fulfillment of any signs.

How do we account for this seemingly anomalous situation? Why has the Lord apparently delayed His return so long?

This is exactly the question that Peter predicted scoffers would be asking in the last days.

> *There shall come in the last days scoffers, walking after their own lusts, And saying; Where is the promise of His coming? for since the fathers fell asleep, all things continue as they were from the beginning of the creation (II Peter 3:3,4).*

But then Peter went on to stress that "the Lord is not slack concerning His promise." The reason He has not already kept His promise is that He is "longsuffering to usward, not willing that any should perish, but that all should come to repentance" (II Peter 3:9). There are still others who need to come to Christ, in repentance and faith, to receive His gift of eternal life.

There are not yet enough residents of the holy city, and He is waiting for us to call others to come. The Lord has prepared a great supper and many already have come, but "yet there is room." Therefore, the Lord is saying to His servants, "Go out into the highways and hedges, and compel them to come in, that my house may be filled" (Luke 14:22,23).

Therefore, if we really "love His appearing," this should be a great incentive for being witnesses unto Him, as He said, "unto the uttermost parts of the earth" (Acts 1:8). As Peter concluded, we can be "looking for and hasting unto [that is 'hastening'] the coming of the day of God." Instead of idling, while we await His return, we should "account that the longsuffering of our Lord is salvation" (II Peter 3:12,15), and do all that we can to bring men to repentance—that is, to get them to change their minds away from being "conformed to this world" (Romans 12:2), and then to bring "into captivity every thought [same word as 'mind'] to the obedience of Christ" (II Corinthians 10:5).

We have been given the Great Commission to "teach all nations," to "preach the gospel to every creature," to "be witnesses unto me ... unto the uttermost part of the earth" (Matthew 28:19; Mark 16:15; Acts 1:8). This has apparently not yet been done, and so the "many mansions" in His Father's house have not yet been filled. Jesus said: "This gospel of the kingdom shall be preached in all the world for a witness unto all nations: and then shall the end come" (Matthew 24:14).

But it does seem that the gospel has indeed been "published among all nations" (Mark 13:10)—or at least nearly so. Missionaries, Bibles, Christian literature, Christian radio, seem now almost to have blanketed the earth, making the gospel at least accessible to those who sincerely desire to know the true God. There may be a few remote tribes not yet contacted, and missionaries are working hard to reach these, but it does seem that at least some out of almost "all nations, and kindreds, and people, and tongues" (Revelation 7:9) have come to know the Lord. Since the Lord is still waiting, there is still more to do, and He has commanded us to "occupy till I come" (Luke 19:13), but His work surely can and should be completed in this generation!

In His great Olivet discourse, after giving the "signs of His coming" (the worldwide state of war, accompanied by famines and pestilences and earthquakes, and also the budding of the Israeli "fig tree," as well as the worldwide proclamation of the gospel), and then giving the outline of the terrible events of the tribulation period followed by His return to earth in power and great glory, Christ made this most significant promise:

> *Verily I say unto you, This generation shall not pass, till all these things be fulfilled. Heaven and earth shall pass away, but my words shall not pass away (Matthew 24:34,35).*

In this striking prophecy, the words "this generation" has the emphasis of "that generation." That is, *that* generation— the one that sees the specified signs of His coming—will not completely pass away until He has returned to reign as King.

Now if the first sign was, as we have surmised, the first World War, then followed by all His other signs, His coming must indeed be very near—even at the doors! There are only a few people still living from that generation. I myself was born just a month before the Armistice was signed on November 11, 1918. Those who were old enough really to know about that first World War—"the beginning of sorrows"— would be at least in their eighties now. Thus, although we cannot be dogmatic, we could very well now be living in the very last days before the return of our Lord!

Throughout all Ages

It may help at this point to place in chronological order the momentous events we have been gleaning from the prophetic Scriptures. The downward trends of the present age will continue and grow worse and worse—morally, spiritually, economically, politically—at the same time that science, technology, and pseudo-education continue to proliferate. The Muslim world and the Middle East will continue in turmoil, eventually boiling over in a sudden invasion of Israel by Russia and her allies among the Muslim nations. A catastrophic providential defeat of this confederacy will leave a political vacuum in the Middle East with Israel awakened out of her atheistic humanism, but still not ready to acknowledge Jesus Christ as her long-awaited Messiah.

A strong alliance of European and other western nations will then quickly become dominant in the world, and one great leader will achieve eminence over the rest. He will probably set up a new capital in rebuilt Babylon, where he hopes to achieve world hegemony. At some point, he and his alliance will have acquired enough power to enable them to make a seven-year treaty with Israel (no doubt over Arab objections) to reestablish their traditional worship in a new temple at Jerusalem. To those who are Biblically literate, this will be recognized as the beginning of Daniel's seventieth week, the seven-year tribulation and the great "day of the Lord."

At some unknown point of time in this series of events (but certainly before the seven-year treaty is set up), the Lord Jesus Christ will descend from heaven to begin His Second Advent. The first event associated with His coming will be the resurrection, immortalizing and catching up of all believers—living or dead—from the age subsequent to His first coming, to meet the Lord in the air, along with all His holy angels and the saints from previous ages.

Then will follow the tribulation period of God's judgments on earth, climaxed by His glorious appearing to destroy the Beast and his hosts at Armageddon in the land of Israel; He will then establish His millennial kingdom on earth, centered at Jerusalem. Those who become believers and are martyred during the tribulation period will also be resurrected and raptured during or after that period, to join all the other redeemed saints of the Lord in the holy city suspended high in the atmosphere over the earth. This latter group of saints in particular, probably joined by all the others, "lived [i.e., 'were resurrected'] and reigned with Christ a thousand years" (Revelation 20:4).

The seven years of judgments on earth will apparently be observed with great interest by the raptured saints with Christ in heaven. There are also some indications (e.g., Revelation 6:16-17; 11:12; 12:6; 14:6,7; 16:11) that people on earth will, to some degree, become aware of the great city hovering over the earth, and of the imminent battle with the returning Christ. They will, nevertheless, continue in their rebellion, following Satan and the Beast until they are all destroyed at Armageddon when Christ comes to earth.

During the thousand-year reign of Christ and His saints over the earth, peace and righteousness will prevail. Then Satan will be unleashed again to lead one last rebellion against God. At this time, the earth will be burned up and then made new again, the judgment of the dead will be accomplished, and the Devil and all the unsaved men and women of all the ages, with all the fallen angels, will be banished forever to the far-distant lake of fire.

It is obvious that, in a book of this size, only the major events of the tribulation and millennium can be surveyed. This outline, however, should suffice for our purposes, and interested students can fill in the details, from the prophetic Scriptures, aided by larger commentaries (e.g., *The Revelation Record*, by this writer). We now wish, however, to look at the eternal ages to come, and our future lives in the New Jerusalem.

We are introduced to our future home and God's eternally new world order in these beautiful words of the Apostle John:

> *And I saw a new heaven and a new earth; for the first heaven and the first earth were passed away; and there was no more sea. And I John saw the holy city, new Jerusalem, coming down from God out of heaven, prepared as a bride adorned for her husband. And I heard a great voice out of heaven saying, Behold, the tabernacle of God is with men, and He will dwell with*

them, and they shall be His people, and God Himself shall be with them and be their God (Revelation 21:1-3).

This is where we shall live in the ages to come, the most beautiful city ever dreamed of, with streets of gold and walls of jasper, gates of pearl and foundations garnished with all manner of precious stones. From the central throne will proceed a river of pure water, bordered with stands of the tree of life, seen briefly once before in God's garden in Eden, trees bearing health-giving leaves and a different fruit every month. The presence of Christ, the Lamb, with the Lord God Almighty, will flood the city continually with light, so that there can be no night there. The sun and moon and stars will exist forever, still in the heavens as before, but the city no longer will need their light.

The city is tremendous in size, and cubical in shape, approximately 1380 miles long, wide and high. Even when it descends to the new earth, its top will extend far into the new heaven, high above earth's present atmosphere, and its base will cover an area almost half that of the United States.

Presumably, its golden streets will stretch vertically as well as horizontally, and we—with our new bodies like that of our Savior—can move rapidly in any direction. There will, indeed, be "many mansions" there, so that every inhabitant may have a vast estate he can call his home. One can calculate that approximately forty billion people have been born into the world since Adam, but only a fraction of these will inhabit the holy city (Matthew 7:13-14). Most people, sadly, will have been consigned to the lake of fire, rather than the new Jerusalem, for their eternal home. If, for example, there are 20 billion people there (there will be many there who were born during the millennium, as well as those who died in infancy or in the womb before birth, in addition to the saints of all the ages), and if they are allotted only, say, 25% of the city's volume for estates and mansions, one can also calculate that there would be an estate for each inhabitant equivalent, on the average, to a huge cubical block with 75 acres on each face of the cube. There will be plenty of room for all who will live there!

But that will be only where we live. "His servants shall serve Him" (Revelation 22:3), and that service might be rendered anywhere in God's infinite universe. There exist out there stars in infinite number and variety, each waiting to be explored and enjoyed in the ages to come. We can never, in this life, bound by gravity and electro-magnetic force systems as we are, develop spacecraft that will carry people to even the nearest star, barely four light years away. Then, however, we shall be like the angels, able to travel through space at unimaginable speeds (the angel Gabriel, for example, was "caused to fly swiftly" from God's throne to Daniel's prayer room, covering this vast distance during the interval from the beginning to the end of his prayer—see Daniel 9:20-21). There will be infinite reaches of space to travel, unending worlds to search out and develop, and eternal time in which to do it all!

Our eternal lives will certainly not be lives of idleness. God has created each of us for a purpose, and our service in this life has been only in preparation for our service there—an apprenticeship, as it were. Our eternal ministry will be assigned to us on the basis of our faithfulness here. "Thou hast been faithful over a few things," we hope to hear Him say, "I will make thee ruler over many things" (Matthew 25:21). "And, behold, I come quickly, and my reward is with me, to give every man according as his work shall be" (Revelation 22:12).

There will, of course, be no evil there of any kind—no hatred, no envy, no hypocrisy, no deceit—for "we according to His promise, look for new heavens and a new earth, wherein dwelleth righteousness" (II Peter 3:13). The very curse on the ground will have been removed (Revelation 22:3), so in the physical realm there will henceforth prevail a law of conservation of entropy as well as conservation of energy.

Furthermore, "God shall wipe away all tears from their eyes; and there shall be no more death, neither sorrow, nor crying, neither shall there be any more pain: for the former things are passed away. And He that sat upon the throne said, Behold, I make all things new" (Revelation 22:4,5). The old will be young again, the lame will be whole again, the weak will be strong again, the blind will see, and the deaf will hear.

Since we shall be like Him, we might also infer that we shall be like Him in "apparent age." He died at 33½ years, in the prime of life, and was recognizable as the same after His resurrection, so perhaps we shall also be made new at such an apparent age, in order to serve Him most effectively. This could mean, too, that those who died at younger ages will, in this time of renewal, mature to similar age. Presumably also, we shall all continue to study and learn, both from God's written Word and His created works, for there is enough in both to occupy us throughout all the ages to come.

We would be presumptuous to try to speculate much beyond this, at least for now. The most glorious prospect of all, of course, is that of being with our Lord Jesus Christ. We may well have opportunity to meet and thank the various angels who have guarded and guided us, as ministering spirits for us as the heirs of salvation (Hebrews 1:14) here in this present life. But we especially anticipate the joy of bowing in thankful worship before the Lamb on the throne, for He suffered and died and endured hell itself, so that we could be saved.

The rest of the joys and opportunities that await us we can learn in due time. "He that spared not His own Son but delivered Him up for us all, how shall He not with Him also freely give us all things?" (Romans 8:32). There is far more there than we can contemplate here. "As it is written, Eye hath not seen, nor ear heard, neither have entered into the heart of man, the things which God hath prepared for them that love Him" (I Corinthians 2:9).

In this life, we have been saved by His grace, kept by His grace and abundantly guided and blessed by His grace. But this is only the hem of the garment, as it were. "In the ages to come, He (will) shew the exceeding riches of His grace in His kindness toward us through Christ Jesus" (Ephesians 2:7).

"Now unto Him that is able to do exceeding abundantly above all that we ask or think, according to the power that worketh in us, Unto Him be glory in the church by Christ Jesus throughout all ages, world without end. Amen" (Ephesians 3:20,21).

Recommended Bibliography

1. Anderson, Sir Robert, *The Coming Prince* (Grand Rapids, MI: Kregel Publishing House, 1954), 311 p.

2. Andrews, Samuel J., *Christianity and Anti-Christianity in Their Final Conflict* (Chicago, IL: Moody Press, 1937), 358 p.

3. Deal, Colin, H., *The Beast and the Arabs* (Rutherford College, NC: End-Time Ministry, 1983), 27 p.

4. Dolan, David, *Holy War for the Promised Land* (Nashville, TN: Thomas Nelson Publishers, 1991), 252 p.

5. Dyer, Charles H., *The Rise of Babylon* (Wheaton, IL: Tyndale House Publishers, 1991), 236 p.

6. Cooper, David L., *Future Events Revealed* (Los Angeles, CA: Biblical Research Society, 1940), 250 p.

7. Hislop, Alexander, *The Two Babylons* (American Edition, New York, NY: Loiseaux Brothers, 1950), 330 p.

8. Jeremiah, David, *Escape the Coming Night* (Dallas, TX: Word Publishing Co., 1990), 240 p.

9. LaHaye, Tim F., *The Beginning of the End* (Wheaton, IL: Tyndale Publishing House, 1972), 173 p.

10. Lawrence, Troy, *New Age Messiah Identified* (Lafayette, LA: Huntington House Publishers, 1991), 200 p.

11. Lindsey, Hal, *The Late Great Planet Earth* (Grand Rapids, MI: Zondervan Publishing House, 1970), 192 p.

12. Marrs, Texe, *Mega Forces: Signs and Wonders of the Coming Chaos* (Austin, TX: Living Truth Publishers, 1988), 265 p.

13. Marrs, Texe, *Millennium* (Austin, TX: Living Truth Publishers, 1990), 270 p.

14. Marrs, Texe, *New Age Cults and Religions* (Austin, TX: Living Truth Publishers, 1990), 351 p.

15. Morris, Henry M., *The Long War Against God* (Grand Rapids, MI: Baker Book House, 1989), 344 p.

16. Morris, Henry M., *The Revelation Record* (Wheaton, IL: Tyndale House Publishers, 1983), 521 p.

17. Morris, Henry M., *Scientific Creationism* (Green Forest, AR: Master Books, 1985), 281 p.

18. Morris, Henry M. and Gary E. Parker, *What Is Creation Science?* (Green Forest, AR: Master Books, 1987), 336 p.

19. Pember, G.H., *Mystery, Babylon the Great* (London: Oliphants Publishers, 1942), 149 p.

20. Smith, Wilbur M., *World Crises and the Prophetic Scriptures* (Chicago, IL: Moody Press, 1951), 149 p.

21. Walvoord, John F., *Armageddon, Oil and the Mid-East Crisis* (Grand Rapids, MI: Zondervan Publishing House, 1990), 234 p.

22. Walvoord, John F., *The Nations in Prophecy* (Grand Rapids, MI: Zondervan Publishing House, 1973), 176 p.

23. Webber, David F., *The Image of the Ages* (Lafayette, LA: Huntington House Publishers, 1991), 158 p.

24. Willmington, Harold L., *Signs of the Times* (Wheaton, IL: Tyndale House Publishers, 1981), 167 p.